"Gorgeous photos — and a hip narrative from a saucy storyteller."
— MTV Associate Producer,
I'm on the Runway Fashion Show

"Jillian Shanebrook's modeling and academic career is wonder woman-like. Her intelligence and sense of adventure amaze us."
— Editor, *Popular* Magazine

"A truly colourful depiction of Jillian's experiences in Asia. This is a brilliant piece of work."
— *MediaCorp* Studios

"An adventure full of the requisite elements: exotic ports, romance, catwalk glamour, tropical danger and even Balinese witchdoctors."
— Editor, *Matra* Magazine

© 2002 Jillian Shanebrook
Second Edition

Published by
Blue Bali Editions
email: books@blue.tc

ISBN 0-615-12050-4

Printed in the USA by United Graphics, Inc., Mattoon, IL
Cover by Think Tank Designs, Singapore

For additional copies of this book, visit jillianshanebrook.com

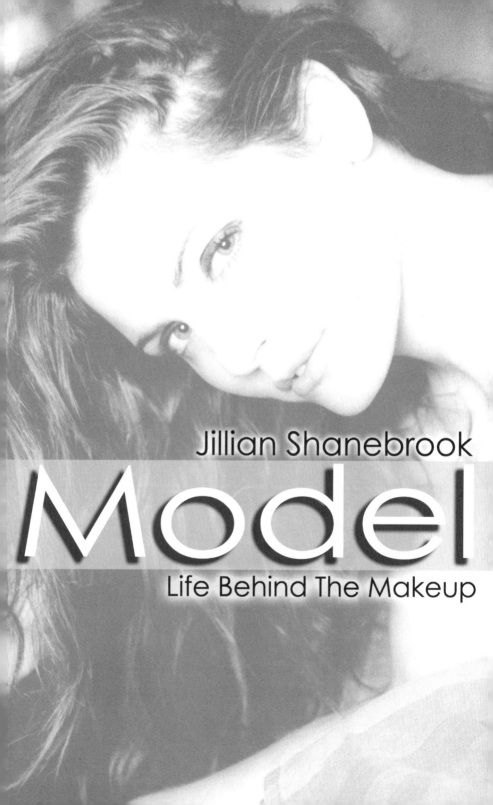

Jillian Shanebrook

Model

Life Behind The Makeup

Contents

To my dear grandfathers
Elwood Alden Eisler and John Abraham Shanebrook
whose spirits always travel with me

Author's Thanks

 I would like to express my deep gratitude to the many people who in their kind generosity made this book possible:

To Thom who joined me on many of these adventures and patiently snapped numerous pictures. To Thomas for the snow and long years of friendship. To Isaac for his brilliant graphic design, photography, and gentle heart. To Greg for listening.

To Ancil for his generous and inspired website design. To my Uncle Bob for his thoughtful photography advice. To Sara for her wise legal counsel.

To Mas Mujimanto and Bu Ani who gave me my start, and to Mas Driego who first encouraged me to write about my adventures. To Yew Kee, my first editor, whose enthusiasm for the initial drafts sustained me through many obstacles and greatly enabled me to write a better book.

To Poay Lim who gave this book life and was an absolute joy to work with. To Wan Ling, my superb editor, who shaped this book up and managed countless duties with such grace.

Thanks to all of my students who have taught me about struggle, integrity, and kindness. To my dear friends Deborah, Kristina, Aramis, Serina, Gretchen, Mark, Doreen, Julie and Bill who are my family and my home, who inspire me everyday with their beautiful souls.

Thanks to Alison, my precious partner in giggles, ashtanga, blah blah, and small pets. Thanks to Gabriel for your wisdom, wit, and Zen philosophy. It is a great joy to have you in my life.

To my parents, Joan and Richard, who motivate me to try to do good, to live a thoughtful and meaningful life. Especially to my Mom for always supporting me in everything I have ever undertaken - I can still hear her yelling "Go Jilly" from the stands at high school track meets. Thanks for always taking that leap of faith. Especially to my Dad for being a rare good man, and for quietly and modestly writing books and papers of immense significance. To my sister Julie, my precious friend, thank you for all your fabulous ideas, tireless energy, incredible instincts - you are one smart woman. And, thanks for all the laughter, advice, and for just being there. These have sustained me and enriched my life more than I can express.

And, thanks to Christopher. Sweet serendipity led me to you, the one I was looking for all along. You so generously gave me your heart – you always had mine.

As far back as I can remember, I have dreamed about the Far East: of wet-green rice fields, fragrances of jasmine and lemongrass, bold empresses, jade mines and bamboo groves. I was charmed by stories of orchid-scented nights, Buddhist monks dressed in saffron robes, and clandestine opium lairs. Little did I know that my fascination with Asia would lead me into the world of international modeling, tropical escapades, stardom, and disastrous crises.

It all started when I hopped on a plane to Indonesia...

Jillian Faith Shanebrook
New York City, February 21, 2002

Indonesian Adventure

New York, April

Dazzling sunshine, electric-pink bougainvillea, and leafy palm trees — these were my first images of Indonesia, described by a friend who had lived on the island of Java. My friend had sipped on coconut and mango fruitshakes, seen smile after smile of warm people, and learned the joyful Indonesian words *Apa Kabar?* (How are you?) Her vivid stories and pictures inspired me to contemplate an Indonesian adventure of my own. I researched volunteer positions in Indonesia and decided to apply to Princeton University, which had a program in Southeast Asia. Some of my friends were surprised: why didn't I just travel there? I explained to them that I didn't want to just spend a few weeks as a tourist. As I had always been fascinated with Southeast Asia, I wanted to live there long enough to capture a sense of everyday life, to live as an Indonesian.

I waited nervously for a couple of months and eventually found out that I was accepted to Princeton and assigned to teach English to Indonesian students in the city of Yogyakarta, on the island of Java, at Gadjah Mada University. I was elated but uneasy. I had never been to this part of the globe and in truth I had little idea if I would actually enjoy the experience. I was about to leave everyone and everything I was familiar with and start a new life.

I flew from New York to Los Angeles, and as I waited to board the plane to Indonesia, I called my friends and family and said my last good-byes — tearful and apprehensive to leave, but in great anticipation of the adventure that lay ahead.

Arrival at Yogyakarta Airport, Indonesia, August 6th

When I first arrived in Yogyakarta, known affectionately as 'Yogya,' I was mesmerized by all of the new sights: *becaks* (bicycle rickshaws), legions of motorcycles, tiny *warungs* (food stalls, assembled and taken apart each day), intense sun, and veiled women, often riding the motorcycles. Outside the city, there were stunningly green padi fields tended to by lean barefooted farmers. I was grateful to have been assigned to Yogya because as one of the centers of Javanese culture, it is home to *wayang kulit* (shadow puppetry), *gamelan* (traditional Indonesian music) orchestras, and classical Javanese dance.

Early mornings in Yogya filled with luminous sunlight were especially enchanting. As soon as I was out of bed, I would step into my garden and breathe in the fragrant air. I was surrounded by orange hibiscus, ginger plants, and banana trees, and serenaded by roosters declaring their place on earth. I would say *Selamat Pagi* (Good Morning) to Mas Mujiran, who took care of my bungalow, and his wife Mbak Titi. They were from a small village nearby, and as soon as I met them, I fell in love with their easygoing personalities; they were usually grinning and laughing about something. Their young daughter, Tiara (already a charmer at three years old), and I would sit for hours in the sun talking a little in English and a little in Indonesian. Breakfasts were great opportunities to sample Indonesia's bountiful variety of fruits. Some of my favorites were fresh *nenas* (pineapple), *jeruk bali* (pomelo), and *belimbing* (starfruit). I also sometimes nibbled on *durian*, a sickly-smelling but tasty fruit. I liked eating it because of its infamous reputation — its pungent odor is so despised that it is even banned from buses and trains in Singapore. Before leaving for school, I was sometimes audience to a roving neighborhood group of musicians who carried tambourines and string instruments and wailed in Javanese.

Before long, I bought a Honda motorcycle (to the dismay of my parents) and felt eager to wander and explore every corner of Yogya. The walled city surrounding the Kraton — the huge palace of the Sultanate of Yogya where people have lived for centuries — became one of my favorite haunts. Riding my motorcycle through the narrow white-walled streets late at night, I often imagined the *saronged* generations that had walked these lanes. I would usually end up near the palace, in an ancient square dominated by a pair of enormous three-hundred-year-old trees. Many Indonesians gather here, attracted by a popular legend that it is impossible to walk a straight line between the trees blindfolded because of fairies who like to trick humans and lure them astray. At night, determined Indonesians blindfold themselves and try to march a straight line; I would join them, taking slow steady steps, resolved to remain straight. I always thought I succeeded until I took off my blindfold and saw that I was far off to one side, sometimes even having made a near circle. I couldn't help but develop a bit of faith in fairy power.

When I wasn't walking around blind-folded, I spent time with my friends — Sophie, a witty teacher also from Princeton; Matt, a rugged Australian graduate student; and Lusi, a bubbly Indonesian college sophomore. The four of us were quite nocturnal and passed many a night singing karaoke down in Sosrowijian (the tourist area of Yogya), lounging in my garden gazing at the stars, and riding our motorcycles out to nearby Prambanan, a Hindu monument built in 900 A.D. On our way to Prambanan, Matt would provide us with a lot of entertainment, Australian-style, as he popped wheelies and yahooed through the silent rice fields. For all-night Javanese culture, we went to the wayang kulit performances in the Kraton.

In wayang kulit, intricate leather puppets are silhouetted onto a white screen and act out traditional stories (for instance, a Javanese Sultan's search for holy water). I didn't usually understand too much since the puppets spoke Javanese — a much more complicated language than the Indonesian I was studying. The stories were accompanied by the haunting sounds of the gamelan orchestra, consisting of hanging gongs, xylophones, finger drums, bronze bowls, and zithers. The sounds are particularly unusual and off-key to Western ears, and extremely eerie and mesmerizing. Gamelan is like music from dreams, full of strange but pleasant sounds moving between high and low pitch unexpectedly. During the all-night performances, I would usually catnap on Lusi's tummy or nibble on *nasi gudeg*, the Yogya specialty of rice and young jackfruit cooked in coconut milk.

I adored Lusi and all of my students. Teaching English to them was a pleasure. Not only did I feel that I was helping them learn something useful, but in turn, they educated me about Indonesian culture: once when I thought I had broken my arm in a motorcycle spill, one of my students suggested that I go to a *dukun* (witch doctor)!

Altogether, my new environment was blissful and enlightening. Indonesia's gracious people and raw beauty amazed me, and any fears I had before I left home evaporated almost immediately. All of the unfamiliar images, smells, and sounds jogged my senses. As I experienced a parallel but alternate lifestyle, I felt the boundaries of what I had known as 'life on earth' expand.

I also felt borders extend in terms of my own life. I realized that living in Indonesia, or in any foreign country where no one knew me, with my family and peers thousands of kilometers away, the image of who I was — my personality, my goals, my role in my community — was also very distant. This afforded the incredible opportunity to recreate myself, to do whatever I pleased, to be whomever I chose.

The Modeling Bug Bites

A few months into my stay, I began to notice that people were watching me on the streets and murmuring about my appearance. I was attracting attention because I was very tall compared to most

Indonesians, and being one of the few Western women there, I had relatively 'exotic' features. I started to toy with the idea of modeling. I remembered how back in the States my friends had encouraged me to try modeling and how agents in New York had given me their cards, but I had never given it a serious thought. At home I was a student, and my identity was wrapped up in the pursuit of knowledge — a view encouraged by my father, a college professor, and my mother, a psychotherapist. For me, success was intelligence, and I worked vigorously towards that goal, graduating second in my college class, *summa cum laude*. Modeling had always seemed like a trivial pursuit. Yet in Indonesia, with the realization that I could try whatever I wanted to and adopt a completely new persona, I thought 'why not try modeling?' I longed to encounter all that life had to offer, and if I failed it would just be a good story and an intriguing experience. So far, 'failures' in my life had taught me at least as much as 'successes.'

One Saturday afternoon a few weeks later, I set out to visit some modeling agencies I had found in the Yogya phone book. I trooped around town with rather disappointing results: many addresses did not exist and the rest were modeling schools, which intuitively seemed like a waste of time and money. I recalled a conversation with a friend who had modeled, and she refused to go to a modeling school on the grounds that the profession can't be 'learned.' The harsh reality is that one either *has* the physical attributes that photographers are looking for or one doesn't. She explained that since so many people want to become models, schools are able to prey on their illusions ("with a little make-up and runway practice you'll be snatched up by any agency") and profit highly.

'Discovered'

A few weeks later I happened to be in the right place at the right time. I went with Matt, my Australian friend, to get his hair cut at the salon of a new grand hotel downtown. He had thought about getting a 'Mohawk' but came to his senses when I described to him what he would be subjecting the citizens of Indonesia to: a burly, 200 cm. Aussie bellowing phrases such as 'fire up the barbie,' with a Mohawk to top the whole ensemble off. It was too much. Indonesians would only run away in horror.

As the hotel salon manager, Pak Majid, snipped away at Matt's hair, giving him a sensible trim, he asked me, "Have you ever modeled before?"

I said no.

"Would you like to be in an upcoming show at the hotel? It's part of the hotel's grand opening."

I hesitated, and then said "Sure."

As soon as I said "Sure," I thought to myself, 'Uh oh, you are really in trouble now, you don't have the slightest idea how to model,' and I regretted my cocky dismissal of modeling schools. Before I had time to change my mind however, Pak Majid sent me over to see the designer for the show, Chaliet Bambang, who would decide whether or not to use me.

I rode my motorcycle over to Bu Chaliet's studio and entered feeling very nervous. It was a smart, stylish space with rows of elegant clothes. I knew I would have to be graceful and as gorgeous as I could be to get this job. Bu Chaliet smiled when she saw me and asked me to put on spiked high heels and walk across the room a few times. I was terrified that I was going to topple over in the heels, but I thought I might be able to pull off the supermodel walk I had often seen in fashion shows: walking very erectly, shoulders back, head high, shaking the hips ever so slightly, tossing the hair seductively, and most importantly, conferring a look of utter indifference and superiority. In all honesty, my girl-friends and I had been doing this walk past schoolboys since age twelve. So I slipped on the heels and sashayed back and forth across the studio. Apparently, years of practice paid off. Bu Chaliet beamed, clapped her hands and told me I was fabulous, and that I was hired and should be at the hotel tomorrow morning because she wanted to use me in newspaper and magazine advertisements for the show. I walked out and breathed a sigh of relief, thinking 'So far, so good.'

The First Photo Shoot

The next day I was at the hotel, overwhelmed by the attention of a small army of men and women. They proceeded to give me a facial, paint my nails, and trim my hair. They put make-up all over my body, including my neck, breasts, and arms. They spent at least an hour on my face, using myriad products just on my lips — toner, pencil, foundation, gloss. They put my hair up in curlers and blow-dried all the curls out ("This will give your hair body"), using a straightening wand to make my hair super slick and shiny. After two hours of near-frenzy, I understood why models look so good. Almost anyone would, given this much attention. I saw myself in the mirror and knew that there was no way I could recreate this image on my own.

I was finally shuttled off to a photo studio, and as I entered and the photographer and his assistants turned to greet me, I felt truly transformed into a model. With gobs of make-up, my face resembled an exotic painting; dressed in a silky short robe and heels, I towered over everyone; and a young assistant was attending to my every need — carrying my water bottle, holding my bag, and keeping my face powdered. The photographer, Mas Arjatmo, led me into a dressing room and told me to try on a sequined gown first. I held my breath as it went over my head, hoping that it would fit decently. (I had no idea if my body would be a proper mannequin for these clothes.) It was a tad snug, but accentuated my 'curves.' A female assistant helped me make the most of my cleavage with the ingenious help of a 'miraclebra.' I walked back out into the studio and Mas Arjatmo sat me down and told me to relax, breathe deeply, and think of myself as the loveliest girl in the world. I took a deep breath, stood up, struck what I hoped was a model pose and he started snapping photos. As he shot he was purring something in Indonesian. And I am pretty sure the translation is something like, "... magnificent, give me another, more, ah sexy ... come on, give it to me ..." (I had to laugh because he seemed to be talking just like the stereotype of a fashion photographer.) I modeled several different outfits that afternoon, the art director sometimes pointing to pages in fashion magazines to direct my poses. I guess all my *Vogue* magazine reading as a teenager had really been studying. It was all fairly effortless. "Now pucker, now sexy pout, now move your body ..." No problem.

A couple of days later I saw myself in the local Yogya newspapers *Minggu Pagi* and *Siang Ini*. There I was, pouting and advertising the fashion show, strangely enough looking like a model.

Walking the Runway

Later that week I was sent to a downtown modeling agency to meet the other models for the show, and start catwalk practice. Walking in to meet a group of models for the first time was very intimidating. After years of compliments in the looks department, I was now surrounded by a group of gene pool champions and I wasn't so special anymore. And I certainly could not rely on the other models to reassure my confidence, they were too busy surveying me — I was ambushed by slow stony looks up and down my body. One of the more self-aware models later explained it to me this way (hardly taking a breath during her explanation):

> *"When you see a new girl, you look at how tall she is, how long her legs are, how large her breasts are. You calculate: is her face beautiful or plain? does she just have a good body? how is her skin? what about her hair? is she a sexy/cute/exotic/girl-next-door type? You want to find a flaw, maybe her nose is too long or her arms have no muscle definition. You want to feel that she is less attractive than you, to give you a feeling of beauty superiority that you are used to in the real world and want to achieve in the modeling world — so that you have a chance to be a supermodel."*

My goodness! This was serious business.

After a few more meetings and a bit more gawking, most of the models eventually became friendly. They asked me questions about New York and if I was a famous model there (which seemed really funny since I was pretty nervous just trying to be a model in Yogya as we learned our routines for the catwalk). Models may look like they are walking naturally on the runway, but we actually memorize proper steps and fairly complicated turns to achieve that effortless-looking saunter. As we practiced our steps that week, I heard from our modeling coach and the other models only words that described my looks, and I started to feel a little depressed. I was treated as if I was just an attractive robot, and no one seemed very interested in what I had to say or what I felt. I started to understand why some models, in an attempt to escape this reality, end up involved in drugs and reckless behavior; the modeling environment can be very dehumanizing, and frankly, a bit boring.

The day of the show arrived and I woke up with a tense stomachache. The other models and I had to arrive at the hotel early for full make-up, and some of the models started to get a little competitive again. A few of them actually pouted when they didn't have the full attention of the stylists. The poor stylists meanwhile were under immense pressure to get everyone ready. As one stylist, Daryanto, was blowdrying my hair, his brush became tangled in my curls. The head stylist treated it as a major catastrophe, yelling and angrily gesticulating at Daryanto who began to look very pale and frightened. As Daryanto slowly untangled my hair, his hands were shaking and he was gravely frowning, as if he had blundered a heart transplant. Yes, beauty was indeed serious business. I also observed how models are truly glorified props with little power or choice. The head stylist wanted one of the girls to have her hair cut short into a bob and streaked red to match a particular outfit. Although the girl did not want to do it, the subtle message was either do it or leave the show. So she had her hair cut — ten years to grow, one stylist and ten minutes to cut it.

After a few hours, everyone looked dazzling and it was time for the catwalk. Walking out on the runway was very empowering. I had memorized my turns and steps, I had been groomed for hours, it was now time, as the other models had taught me, to 'flaunt it.' Yet there were a couple of things to keep in mind: one was staying upright in my high heels, and the other was running backstage fast enough to change clothes for my next walk. Backstage was a flurry of naked models, clothes flying overhead, breasts being taped (a trick to achieve maximum cleavage), and assistants running around zipping, fastening, and primping. Pak Majid was yelling various directives including "Hurry," "Don't rip that skirt," "Get your hair down," "Put on these earrings," and "Smile!"

Out in the audience, there was a battalion of photographers lining the sides of the runway. I had never been subjected to so many camera flashes before and I was initially concerned I might be partially blinded and totter off the stage. There also appeared to be lots of 'ladies who lunch' sitting in the front rows of the audience. The reaction of the crowd was mixed — some people were expressionless, others were grinning and appeared encouraging. The photographers generally served as veritable cheering squads and were extremely enthusiastic. A few even googly-eyed a bit. (Of course it was in their best interest to flatter us this way because we would be more likely to pause for their cameras.)

I found the runway setup an interesting, almost confrontational dynamic, especially with women. Women have such complicated relationships with 'beauty.' Given the importance society places on beauty, it's not surprising that some women react strongly (comparing themselves with the models, feeling envious, sometimes just disassociating) when models are literally 'put on a pedestal' largely for their looks. Some embrace the spectacle, others do not. I had certainly felt envious plenty of times watching models parade around.

For the final walk, Pak Majid selected me to wear the crowning fashion creation solo down the runway (I believe it was a slinky pantsuit). It was a strange feeling being up there by myself, in this new role, as a model. Honestly, I felt like an impostor, or more accurately, an observer, watching people watch me, 'the model.' I was looking for Matt, Sophie, and Lusi in the audience but I couldn't find them. It turned out they came just as the show finished because I had mistakenly told them to come an hour late. My big debut, and no friends to see it. After the show ended I felt very pumped up from all the attention. A luncheon followed, which included a karaoke DJ, and in my jazzed-up condition I took the stage to sing but didn't receive quite the same positive feedback as I had earlier. One thing at a time ...

Afterwards, some of the models, my friends, and I went out for *Padang* food, super-*pedas* (spicy) food from the *Minangkabau* people in Sumatra. Padang must be the world's fastest fast food: there isn't a menu, you just sit down and a dozen bowls suddenly appear. You only pay for the empty bowls and sampling is free. We gorged on *rendang* (beef and buffalo meat slowly cooked in coconut milk), various curries, vegetables, fish, eggs, and rice. The food was so *pedas* that it burned our fingers and we plunged them into bowls of cool water placed strategically for that purpose. After dinner, Matt and I were chatting about my possible modeling career and he teased, "Do you think they'd have any use for a roguish Aussie on the catwalk?" I told him I thought he would look charming in the pantsuit I had worn earlier, and he said he would start waxing his legs and parading around the house in heels. Meanwhile, Lusi was resting her head on Matt's shoulder, exhausted after eating so much.

First Lady Visit

After my first runway experience, I felt very grateful for the adventure that my life in Indonesia was affording me. Another intriguing opportunity presented itself a few weeks later — the American Embassy contacted Gadjah Mada University, explaining that Hillary Clinton was vacationing in Yogya. As Sophie and I were among the few fellow Americans in Yogya, we were invited to spend a day with Hillary sight-seeing. *Bagus ya*.

A couple of days later we met Hillary and were shocked by the amount of security for her, as a busload of Secret Service men followed us around everywhere we went. The entire entourage first visited an elementary school, and then Borobodur, one of the triumvirate of famed Southeast Asian Buddhist monuments (along with Angkor Wat in Cambodia and Bagan in Myanmar). Ascending the huge monument represents rising through the ten mental stages towards spiritual enlightenment. The day concluded in nearby Kota Gede, a village renown for its fine silver. The whole day, Hillary was playful, curious, and very impressed with Yogya and its environs. As Hillary and I said good-bye, I told her "I'm thrilled to have such a strong woman in the White House."

She looked at me with a smile. "Thanks and don't forget your absentee ballot while you are living here." She was certainly a consummate pro, not missing a chance to gain one more vote for her political career.

Bali

Over the next couple of months I appeared in many more fashion shows, including a beauty workshop in which my hair was curled into dozens of ringlets. With the hairdo, Sophie thought I bore a striking resemblance to her cocker spaniel back in the States and at one point petted my head and cooed, "Scooter." Eventually needing a break from modeling, I decided to do a bit of traveling in Bali since so many of my friends had raved about its beauty. Matt came along, and we set off from Java by bus. I was very happy to sit next to him, just to listen to his delicious Aussie accent, especially as he greeted other passengers with a roaring "G'day mate!" Matt spent most of the trip telling me about growing up in the Australian outback, where crocodiles and kangaroos are as common as cats and dogs. He said he never had any problems with the 'crocs' or the 'roos,' but he and his brother would often have to shoot copperhead and king snakes slithering up their porch steps. Matt also gave me a preview to Bali since he had been there before, explaining that Bali is the only Hindu community in predominantly Islamic Indonesia, and according to some, has more Hindu temples than people. Bali is also home to picturesque padi fields, Balinese dancing girls, and turquoise waters with schools of gentle dolphins.

Kuta and Ubud

After a ten-hour ride, we finally arrived in Bali and went straight to Kuta Beach, known for its surf and sunsets, to take a swim. We were surprised to see a traditional Balinese funeral procession along the shore. There were musicians beating on cymbals and drums, and at least one hundred people marching slowly, wearing white and yellow sarongs, and holding ornamental golden umbrellas. We watched for a few minutes and then out of respect for their privacy, we left the beach, heading towards the town of Kuta. Kuta is the first stop in Bali for many young travelers, as its nightlife is incredibly active, certainly the hottest spot in all of Indonesia. After several months in cultural but quiet Yogya, Matt and I were very keen to mix, mingle, flirt, and dance. We went straight to The Bounty, a club built in the shape of a sailing ship, and saw the zealous international crowd that had gathered, including Europeans, Australians, Japanese, as well as local Balinese guys and girls. There were so many big Australian boys and I spent most of the evening chatting with a group of Aussie surfers. Our conversation was sprinkled with surf talk — waves were 'rad,' 'gnarly,' and 'bogus.' One of the surfers, Qualey, was a crawfisherman on the north coast of Australia, and he described his life sailing out into the deep sea every day and hauling up his catch. His existence seemed so simple and uncomplicated compared to the chaotic urban one I had left behind in the States. He invited me to go out on his trawler and I thought I would definitely take him up on it the next time I was in Queensland.

From Kuta, Matt and I traveled north up to Ubud, the artistic center of Bali, where there is an abundance of Balinese arts, handicrafts, dance, and music. Ubud was one of the most enchanting places I have ever been: there were glistening green rice fields, tinkling streams, and at night captivating sounds of crickets and other critters like *cecak* (small lizards) chirping and idling in the grasses. If heaven exists, it will hopefully be as tranquil and magical as Ubud. Matt and I went to see the *Legong* dance, a dance for girls between eight and thirteen, considered the finest and most feminine of Balinese dances. The young girls dressed in colorful silk and wearing elaborate headdresses decorated with frangipani flowers entranced us. They cocked their faces at sharp angles and twirled their slender fingers gracefully, keeping them straight and taut, with their thumbs inward against their palms. A woman seated next to us explained that the movements are so regimented and difficult to master that the girls start training at a very young age until "dance enters their innermost beings." After the Legong dance, we walked along a scenic lane through rice fields to spend the night at the magnificent Amandari Hotel, set high above the Ayung River. Our bungalow had its own orchid garden, personal servants, and a pool. Matt and I stayed up chatting about our Indonesian lives, eating sate and drinking *es campur*, a bizarre but *enak* (delicious) mixture of fruit, milk, and crushed ice. It was one of those evenings that spilled over far into the next morning and I felt as if I had really lived a night.

Amed

From Ubud we headed onto eastern Bali, a much more arid region, to a small fishing village near the town of Amed. We found a little inn by the sea, and after settling in, I sat out in the late afternoon sun listening to mysterious gamelan music on my walkman. I could see dozens of quiet blue sail boats coming back from the day's fishing, and nearby a young Balinese woman was making the nightly Hindu offerings of flowers and incense. I felt I was very far from home, in a strange and mystical place ...

That night, Matt and I met a Dutch painter and his wife who had been coming to Bali for twenty years. Over dinner, they told us a very eerie story. Many years ago they were traveling from northern Bali towards the south with their two daughters and a Balinese driver. As darkness crept upon them, they started looking for a place to rest for the night and eventually came across a small village in the mountains. The driver seemed uneasy and told them he didn't think it was a suitable place to stop. But as their girls were tired and hungry, they asked the driver to pull over, and they got out of the car and asked the villagers for some food and a place to sleep. The villagers also seemed uneasy but gave them some rice and showed them to a small hut for shelter. The family and the driver ate the rice, but the night was very cold and they all had trouble falling asleep. In the middle of the night, as the wife lay tossing and turning, she saw an old woman, long-haired and dressed in a purple sarong, pacing in the distance and staring at their hut. She felt very disturbed and frightened by the woman's presence but she did not want to alarm her husband or her daughters so she kept what she saw to herself.

Morning finally came, and they were all exhausted but relieved to leave the village and complete their journey to Kuta. Their relief soon turned to panic though, as there was something very wrong with their younger daughter. She was sweating profusely, had a high fever, and most disturbingly, she was mumbling in Balinese, a language completely foreign to her! Her parents were absolutely shocked and tried talking to her in Dutch, but she only responded in Balinese. They carried her to the car, and by the time they reached Kuta, she was nearly unconscious. They were desperate, not understanding what could have possibly happened to their daughter. Finally, upon the advice of their Balinese driver, they called in a *guruji* (Hindu priest). Over the next several days, he performed exorcisms on the little girl. I tried to ask them what exactly happened during the exorcisms but they both became quiet and looked very pained, obviously not wanting to remember. They said only that their daughter recovered and did not recall anything of the incident, never speaking in Balinese again. They believe that their daughter was possessed by the old woman, who may have been a dukun and furious about having foreigners lodge in her village.

After saying *Selamat Malam* (Good Night) to my Dutch friends and Matt, I went back to my dark room alone, thinking about all the mysteries that lay in this huge land of Indonesia, and how I hoped not to run into too many horrifying ones. I felt very spooked that my room was cold and that the wind howled throughout the night. Even though I knew the chances were slim, I was fearful I might see an old woman outside my window.

15

Magazine Cover Story

I awoke the next day thrilled to hear only English and not Balinese from Matt and I. When we returned to Yogya, a fax from *Popular Magazine* (which is also the 'most popular' men's magazine in Indonesia) had arrived in my absence, inviting me to Jakarta for a photo shoot and cover story. This was a very interesting development: before I left for Bali I had been growing a little antsy just doing fashion shows and had sent Popular some photos with the intent of starting to do some editorial work. I didn't have much faith that I would actually hear from the magazine, but I wanted to at least create the possibility. With Popular's invitation, I finally realized that a 'star' is created, not born. (I guess I had always assumed women on magazine covers had some kind of covergirl birthright. I never imagined that *I* could end up on a cover.) What fascinated me was that I hadn't done anything remarkable — I had walked down a few runways, I was attractive, but certainly not the most beautiful girl in Indonesia. In short, there was no clear reason why I deserved this invitation, except for the fact that I had sent in some photographs, and they must have arrived at a fortuitous time, catching someone's eye. They needed a covergirl and there were my pictures lying on the editor's desk. I recognized that a person becomes prominent or 'successful' in modeling (or in any other industry) through their own perseverance and a healthy dose of good timing, or bluntly put, blind luck.

Popular's cover story would generate publicity for me. And publicity, more than anything a person does, is what works to create a 'star.' (Positive publicity is good, but sometimes negative publicity works just as well.) Look at Madonna, one of the most well known entertainers in the world. If she had performed as usual (singing, dancing, acting controversially), but did so without a camera or a journalist to record her activities, who would she be? She would be a performer, but not a star. Even our current obsession with reality TV shows illustrates the gargantuan role of publicity — the people on the shows often become famous just for being in the public eye, not necessarily for anything they have done.

But given all these thoughts, the truth was that I felt very excited about the cover story — I accepted Popular's invitation and made arrangements to fly to Jakarta.

Arrival at Sukarno-Hatta International Airport, Jakarta, April 5th

As I landed in Jakarta, I thought back to my first night there when I had a stopover on my way from L.A. to Yogya. I never would have imagined that my next visit would be for a magazine cover story. I had definitely begun to re-create myself. I was picked up at the airport by a young editorial assistant and taken to the headquarters of Popular where I met Mas Mujimanto, the senior editor, and Bu Ani, the associate editor. I was given a grand tour — introduced to some past covergirls, shown a poster collection of Popular 'bathing beauties,' and then fitted in dozens of rather skimpy bathing suits. Bu Ani interviewed me, with breezy questions usually found in mainstream magazines, including "What do you like about Indonesia?", "What are your future goals?", and "Where is your favorite vacation spot?"

Then Mas Mujimanto took me out to lunch in downtown Jakarta at a Japanese restaurant. I started to feel like a 'covergirl' as I turned heads in the restaurant (of course I was wearing a very attention-getting mini-skirt which had become part of my modeling 'uniform') and talked about the upcoming shoot and cover story. After lunch, Mas Mujimanto drove me through Jakarta, a contradictory city of great wealth and deep poverty. We drove by huge, corporate buildings that overwhelmed nearby neighborhoods of small shacks. There were super-highways clogged with Mercedes and Range Rovers, towering over groups of tiny warungs below. We passed by Sunda Kelapa, the old Dutch Port that had legions of antiquated schooners. We saw the *Buginese Makasar*, a massive vessel native to Sulawesi, built from the strong timbers of the island and able to withstand the rough seas of the region.

These vessels have always played a colorful role in Indonesia's spice trade. Well before the first European explorers arrived in their pursuit of spices, the Buginese Makasar schooners were carrying cargo and spices to and from the 13,000 islands in the Indonesian archipelago. Yet when the Dutch came and the Bugis Makasar Sultans refused to submit to their domination, the Bugis Makasar sailors were branded as 'pirates' — quite ironically, as the title applied far more accurately to the Dutch.

Cover Photo Shoot

The next day I set out with Bu Ani and the Popular crew — an art director, photographer, and a stylist — for a long weekend of shooting for the cover story pictorial. An Indonesian starlet, Layla, whom I had often seen in her popular television show on RCTI (Rajawali Citra Televisi Indonesia, a major Indonesian network) came as well. She would also be featured in an edition of Popular. We were headed to the seaside resort town of Anyer on the northern coast of Java. The road north was bumpy and curvy and I was sure I was going to be sick in the van, not very becoming for a covergirl. In addition to the rough road, I also felt nauseous from a touch of nerves. Our group included a television star, a whole crew from the top magazine in the country, and little me, a studious college student just a few months before, given the responsibility of carrying a whole magazine edition by myself. I finally calmed my mind by realizing I just had to try and act out the role I had taken on, that of a covergirl.

The next day, once the shooting started, I had regained my confidence and I played my role enthusiastically, smiling and performing for the camera. We spent most of the time on the ocean, with Layla and I taking turns posing on a yacht, kayak, jetskis, and a windsurfer. At one point, there was a tiny bit of 'star behavior.' (I was hoping that something juicy would happen, like Layla refusing to come out for a shoot until she bathed in Dead Sea water flown in by private jet.) Late in the afternoon, Layla seemed distressed with the shoot and retreated back to her private bungalow, later emerging on her cell phone. (In the celebrity pecking order, she had her own bungalow, while I shared one with Bu Ani.) She had also brought along either her agent or her personal assistant who doubled as her hairstylist (I did my own hair — which ended up looking pretty dismal!) All in all though, she was friendly and when I saw her on television a few weeks later I have to admit that I felt excited — I was keeping company with the 'stars.'

Shortly after, the magazine arrived on the newsstands and there I was on the cover, on every kiosk throughout the archipelago, in a nation of nearly 200 million people. Inside, the cover story was over a dozen pages with a multitude of photographs, describing me as an 'upcoming sensation' in Indonesia. The entire affair was surreal — was I on my way to becoming famous? Was this all there was to being famous?

I went to my local newsstand to buy extra copies and the clerk was very surprised to notice I was the young woman on the cover. I quickly attracted a crowd and started signing autographs. My main thought as I stood there signing magazines was how strange it was that someone would desire my signature, and I lamented that my usual signature didn't really have any 'flair.' Caught up in the ridiculousness of the moment, I resolved to practice it, to create a more glamorous-looking autograph. (Luckily, I soon got over this silly idea.) The whole experience felt like some kind of fluke, just a strange situation I had found myself in.

Shoot in Malaysia

Soon after my cover shoot, I was contacted by a producer based in New York City who had seen some of the photos from the Popular cover story. He was shooting a commercial in Malaysia, needed an American model for a role, and invited me to play the part. Intrigued by the idea of an international shoot and the chance to visit Malaysia, I quickly accepted. My flight included a layover in Singapore. I would first stop there and visit my college friend, Lily, and then together we would travel into Malaysia.

Swinging Singapore

Arrival at Changi Airport, Singapore, April 27th

Long before I moved to Indonesia, I had heard all about Singapore from my Singaporean college roommate, Lily. With Lily's gorgeous looks, wit, and affection for her country, I quickly fell in love with her and her island city. As I flew in on Singapore Airlines, carefully pampered by a troop of stylish and articulate Singaporean women who reminded me of Lily, I couldn't help but think that they were some sort of female super-race. (Didn't at least one starlet use to hand out Singapore Airlines peanuts?)

As I stepped off the plane in Singapore I felt a little anxious. I had already carefully read up on 'the rules' of proper Singapore etiquette but what if I forgot and asked to buy chewing gum, or jaywalked (which in NY is *de rigueur* if you want to get anywhere). Would I really be caned? Hmmm, sounded kind of kinky. I double-checked my purse (the night before I had inspected it for gum) and found to my horror one small piece of Wrigley's Spearmint. I quickly glanced around and surreptitiously swallowed the offender, vowing from now on to be on my best behavior.

City of Orchids and Bougainvillea

Lily met me at Changi, radiant as ever with her long glossy black hair and sassy Vera Wang suit. I would stay in Singapore for a couple of days and then Lily and I were going to road-trip through Malaysia, first stopping on the east coast so I could film the commercial. As we hopped into her chauffeur-driven Jaguar and were whisked towards her house, I gleefully reveled in my first sightings of Singapore. I thought it was grand, like New York City, but new, green, and clean. There were elegant colonial buildings and ultra-modern skyscrapers rising out of a garden of lush tropical plants, including chartreuse and mauve orchids and shocking peach bougainvillea. Even the country's name is melodious, Sing-a-pore. We passed by the Padang across from the magnificent St. Andrews Cathedral and Lily said cricket matches are often held there, with the players dressed in crisp, white uniforms. Observing the people on the street, I thought about the richness of Singaporean culture — the Malays, Chinese, and Indians who have each brought centuries of history and customs from their homelands, as well as the past generations and influences of British colonialists, pirates, and man-eating tigers.

As we neared Lily's house, Lily said that her neighborhood, Katong, used to be home to lemongrass farms and coconut factories in the nineteenth century. Today, it is the residence of mostly Eurasian and *Peranakan* families. Lily explained that the Peranakans are a community that developed from the frequent intermarrying between the Chinese and the Malays. Peranakan society reached its heyday in the nineteenth century as Chinese men immigrating in search of a better life commonly married local Malay women. Lily said that her mother's *laksa* — the tangy coconut soup which has both Chinese noodles and Malay spices — is an example of the blending of Chinese and Malay tastes that have formed Peranakan culture. When we reached Lily's beautiful terraced mansion, I could see the influence of Malay and Chinese styles: there were vividly painted tiles and delicate green *nyona* porcelain, complimented by embroidered scarlet wall hangings and dark carved furniture inlaid with mother of pearl. It was a Saturday and Lily's

elegant mama was entertaining some ladies on their sunny verandah. They were chattering in Mandarin, fanning themselves, and
playing *mah jong*.

Lily settled me into a guest room and her maid brought us
some iced tea. I lounged on the bed while Lily waltzed around the
room giving me a fashion show. She had stopped by Orchard
Road before the airport, picking up a few outfits to make sure we
were both well-suited for an evening at the hippest nightclub in
town, Zouk. We completely dolled ourselves up — donning little
black dresses with plunging necklines, and then rubbing sparkles
over our blooming busts. Lily also suggested trying some *jamu*
(traditional herbal medicine) with a raw egg, telling me somewhat
shyly that it helps to ensure sexual potency. I didn't think we
needed help in that department but I joined her in sisterly support.
The jamu tasted dreadful but Lily giggled and said, "No pain, no
gain *lah*!" Before going to Zouk, we were first going to meet Lily's
brother and his friend (both E.R. residents at Singapore General
Hospital) for a drink, and I insisted on going to Raffles Hotel.

Raffles

As Lily's chauffeur drove us through the tropical evening, we were
both feeling frisky. So we opened up the large sunroof of the car
and took turns standing up, drinking in the night air. I relished
speeding through the fragrant, balmy darkness in a country I had
yet to discover. It was one of those moments when all is right, and
time stops for a little while, granting us a chance to be grateful
for simply being alive. As we pulled up to the famed hotel, we
collected ourselves, and entered the magnificent hallway, finding
our way into the world-famous Long Bar. There were rattan
chairs, saronged hostesses, and *punkahs* (hanging fans) leisurely
turning, creating an air of colonial gentility. Lily spotted her
brother, Henry, and his colleague, Alex, both dashingly charming
in a Chow Yun Fat way. We sat down, and I knew it was tacky, but
I just had to order a Singapore Sling. The others looked at me as
if I were a country bumpkin and coolly requested gin and tonics.

When the drinks arrived, I sipped up the pink froth, thinking about the sumptuous colonial lifestyle of days gone by, and I quoted James Michener, "To have been young and had a room at Raffles was probably life at its best." Without missing a beat Alex winked and said, "Well, let's all get a room *lah*!"

Conversation soon centered on Singapore magic potions. I mentioned that Lily and I had drunk that despicable jamu concoction and Alex started to laugh and said that jamu, and other remedies, such as Jamaican Irish Moss, have become popular with some of his friends who hope to increase their virility. He said that one of his friends had an excruciatingly embarrassing talk with his father who wanted to ensure his son's 'potency,' and suggested that he wear baggy pants and have ice cube therapy to stimulate his nether regions. Henry laughed and said that when it comes to virility, Singapore guys do not have any problems. Furthermore, they are amazingly resourceful in finding romantic privacy: if they can't get their own HDB flat (government-subsidized public housing), they just take their date out to Fort Canning or Mount Faber.

Zouk

We finished our drinks and drove over with the boys to Zouk, a very swanky disco. We took in the Mediterranean whitewashed architecture, tiered balconies, house music, and young women in leopard skin catsuits prowling around (perhaps imitating a certain starlet's outfit on the night she was discovered here). Lily was the belle of the ball, doing the European double-cheek kiss with Elite models, Aussie and Brit expats, and a group of young women whom she later told me are known as SPGs or Sarong Party Girls (a class of seductresses with a reputation for dating foreign men). Lily also pointed out some TCS (Television Corporation of Singapore — Singapore's only television station) stars, and said there was recently a big hullabaloo that TCS stars should be paid more because they were having to find part-time office jobs. There were guys with chokers, pierced body parts, and platform shoes, and elegant, black-leathered, red-lipsticked Singapore girls. These folks were styling. Alex and Henry introduced me to some boys from their cricket club — all the British influence was fascinating. (Some Americans, myself included, harbor a secret lust for things British.)

We ducked into the Velvet Underground (another famous club) next door (where Lou Reed himself would have liked the thumping music and the velvet-covered walls) and I saw a totally gorgeous creature on the dance floor. He looked Malay and had long black hair, which was kind of a relief in this land of neat short haircuts. And he had rhythm — mercy! He swayed to the beat swinging his mane of hair like a proud lion. Lily saw me staring, and said *"Wah, he's a Mat Rocker!"* She said that 'Mat Rockers' are a subculture of Malay boys with rock-and-roll looks who groove to Deep Purple and Led Zeppelin. They have their own style and lingo, and with a plethora of clean-cut guys in Singapore, she too thought they were totally delicious. I walked up to him and explained that I was American and curious if he was a Mat Rocker. He kindly explained that the name 'Mat Rocker' is a bit insulting coming from an outsider, but it is used within the community. He said that he and his friends are into music and just want to have a place in Singaporean society, to be heard as a minority. I ended up dancing with him, and not only did he seriously outclass me with his soulful moves, he charmed me with his sweet slow dance.

Chinatown

The next morning, Lily took me to Chinatown, and frankly I was more eager to get to Little India because NYC has a huge Chinatown, but no Little India, only a row of Indian restaurants in the East Village. But within a few minutes I realized this Chinatown was certainly not to be missed: there were antiquated colonial shop-houses, narrow streets, and smells of bean cakes and pork dumplings. Lily hired a *trishaw* (a three-wheeled rickshaw) to take us around, and we first went to an herbal shop where the owner gave us a tour of holistic medicine, including dried seahorses and a tiny ginseng root that cost $800 Singapore dollars. (And this for sexual prowess — so many concoctions for virility!) We also stopped by a shop that specializes in papier-mâché goods in the form of snazzy red cars, huge televisions, and karaoke sets. These paper consumer items are burned at funerals so that they can be sent along with the dead for use in the next life. Sounds like a pretty good deal, which leads one to wonder — why not just take it easy this lifetime and stock up on monopoly money for the next life ...

A little while later, still in our trishaw, we heard birds singing and suddenly found ourselves next to a lovely bird concert. Lily said that every Sunday morning, hundreds of Chinese men bring their birds in ornate cages to Chinatown, hanging them overhead on bird-cage stands so the birds can sing together. There were *sharmas, thrushes, mata putehs,* and *merboks,* and their owners sat and chatted, sipping tea and glowing with parental pride. Once in a while a man would get up and move his bird to a different spot, as if looking for the perfect neighbors to accompany his bird's song. After so much sight-seeing we stopped for a snack of *dim sum,* greedily munching on dumplings, stuffed mushrooms puffs, and spiced spare ribs.

Little India

For our first taste of Little India, we traveled up Serangoon Road. Lily said it is one of the oldest roads in Singapore, marked on old maps as "the road through the island." I was brimming with anticipation because I had never been to India before, and I wanted to experience Indian culture. We turned into cozy little streets and saw mounds of spices, newsstands with Indian *Bollywood* magazines, and a trained parrot who could pick your fortune from a deck of cards. We could smell burning sandalwood incense as well as flower garlands which were hanging every-where, fashioned from roses, marigolds, and jasmine. We stopped into a *sari* shop, and I tried on a red, gold-flecked sari together with a *choli* (the short blouse worn with the sari). The exhibitionist in me liked how I could show a little belly. There were piles of silks and Indian women with their exotic *pottu* (the red dot on the forehead — traditionally worn by married Hindu women but recently popular with single Indian women and foreigners as a form of fashion accessory). I could imagine that I was in the bazaars of Delhi or Madras. Next we visited 'Curry Row' (a row of two-story shop-houses made famous by its curry restaurants) and saw some diners enjoying fish head curry. Lily said it is a very popular dish but I couldn't imagine eating with a pair of floating eyeballs staring up at me. I settled for some *gulam jamun* (cream cheese balls) and home-made *thairu* (yogurt) from a street vendor.

Next we headed further north up to the Hindu Sri Srinivasa Perumal temple. We arrived at the temple and were admiring the intricate carvings and strings of mango and coconut leaves when a young man approached us and told us that the fruit leaves are to welcome and purify visitors. He introduced himself as Ramesh, and asked us if we knew about the famous festival that takes place at this temple. I said no, and he told us a hair-raising tale about the Festival of Thaipusam. The festival occurs in late January and offers an opportunity for Hindus who seek forgiveness, wish to fulfill vows, or want to give thanks by performing dangerous feats. One of the feats is a fire-walking ceremony, where the devoted, swathed in yellow cloth as a symbol of holiness, walk across hot coals. After surviving the crossing, they cool their feet in a vat of cow milk. For the truly pious, there is a very intense ritual in which the devoted go into a trance and walk for several kilometers supporting intricate, decorative steel cages (*kavadi*) which are attached to their *bare* skin with hooks. Throughout the parade route, steel skewers are stuck through their cheeks and tongues, supposedly causing no bleeding and leaving no trace of wounds. Ramesh said these feats are endured simply by the power of the mind. Oh my, I certainly hope the devout receive bountiful blessings for braving that torture. I couldn't help but look at the Indian men walking around and wonder if one day they would be sticking rods through their handsome cheeks.

I was in a bit of a daze thinking about these painful rituals as Lily told me that there is also a seedy side to Little India. In an area called Pink Street, there is a red-light district where transvestites congregate ... There was surely no dearth of intriguing sights.

Sentosa

After our intense morning, Lily wanted to take me shopping on Orchard Road, but I declined. Even though I was modeling clothes, I didn't like looking for them. I found shopping extremely tedious. Fortunately, I was starting to acquire most of my wardrobe from the generosity of fashion designers. So Lily went to pick up some Anna Sui alterations and I took the cable car out to Sentosa and met Alex for a quick round of golf. After nine holes, I edged out Alex who claimed the sun was in his eyes during every shot. He said that this was an emasculating defeat for him and jokingly proposed an arm-wrestling match. I told him he could show me what a man he was by carrying me on his back all the way to the cable car station. He agreed, and after a lovely ride holding onto Alex's muscular chest, we caught the cable back and eventually met up with Lily and Henry on Orchard Road.

Night Safari

Henry wanted us to check out an Eric Khoo[1] film but Lily said that they really should take me to the Night Safari. Henry, such an accommodating older brother, said, "Okay *lah*."

A short time later at the Night Safari, Lily and I had somehow lost the boys, and we were walking along in the darkness, a pale

---

1 Eric Khoo — a young Singaporean filmmaker trained in Australia, known for his critically acclaimed and sometimes controversial short films. One of his films *Pain* (a compelling story of a man's fascination with pain) was banned in Singapore but won the Best Director award at the 1994 Singapore International Film Festival.

moon dimly lighting our way and illuminating the wild beasts nearby — cape buffaloes, striped hyenas, golden jackals, and one-horned rhinoceroses. We could hear the animals grunting, howling, and buzzing, and we could sense their nature, wild and feral. Among the cacophony of sounds surrounding us, we suddenly heard deep bellows. The bellows slowly began to dominate the other sounds and the rest of the animals fell silent. The air was still, the bellows unrelenting. Up ahead, from the direction of the noise, Lily and I saw the bushes rustling and our hearts jumped. This was it. Perhaps a rhinoceros was loose, ready to secure a nighttime snack. I quickly looked around, thinking that Lily and I could scale a palm tree to escape the impending danger. But before we could really react, the bellowing creature revealed itself — more buffoon than beast, it was a rather non-intimidating sight. Alex and Henry, besides laughing their heads off, were gamely trying to charge at us. Lily teased that the bellows were part of a courtship ritual between the two.

We kept a close eye on them after that and as we continued to walk around, Alex said that he was pleased he was able to come out to the Night Safari as he liked the fresh air and the animals. His parents had really pressured him to go on a singles harbor cruise (the 'love boat') that night, and he narrowly escaped. He said his mother had signed him up with the SDU (Singapore Development Unit — a government agency created to play matchmaker among Singapore singles) because she wanted to make sure he ended up with a college-educated wife and not with any of the "silly girls" he sometimes dated. Alex said morosely that SDU stands for one thing: Single, Desperate, and Ugly, and he had been trying to avoid every cruise, barbecue, and dance they sponsored. The SDU, according to these boys, is intent on marrying everyone off, and especially bent-on making educated matches — there have been separate mass weddings for groups of couples with 'O' level qualifications and 'A' level qualifications.

I asked Henry if there was any encouragement to enjoy a 'liberating' singles lifestyle. Henry replied that the Singapore government is singularly concerned about the aging population and low birthrates. Therefore they encourage Singapore singles to 'merge, marry, and multiply.' I told them that in the U.S., the government is completely uninvolved in matchmaking, partly because it would prefer to slow down population growth. Henry explained that in Singapore there is significant government entanglement. In addition to the SDU, a book came out not long ago called *Sing Singapore* which Henry said included a verse to encourage women to procreate: "We have the ova in our bodies, we can conceive, we can conceive. We have a role for Singapore, we must receive, we must receive!" I could not imagine Singapore's sophisticated citizenry chanting that rather blunt call for impregnation. Henry chuckled and confessed that he made up the song, but we couldn't help admire the government's concerted effort in their unending quest for increased island city offspring.

Hawker Center

After all the beasts and marriage chatter, we fueled up at the Newton Food Center. This was major excitement — so much food, so little time. Lily told me that Singaporeans can eat twice a day for months without repeating a single dish. I tried *chai tow kueh* and *kelinga mee*, and I loved the bustling, no-frills, the-food-is-the-main-attraction atmosphere. Lily said other spots for delectable dining include Punggol — famous for its fresh crabs, the Satay Club, and her mom's kitchen, where Peranakan nyona cuisine is served.

For dessert, Alex joked that if we ordered durian we should be careful because as a *yang* food it is a powerful aphrodisiac. He said there is a saying in Malaysia "When the durians come down, the sarongs go up," and surveys show that the birth rate in Malaysia takes a jump approximately nine months after the durian season (there are two a year, in June/July and November/December).

Singapore Spying

After eating, I proposed a slightly mischievous activity. I suggested driving out to Fort Canning to observe the romancers. "*Bagus* or not?" "Okay *lah*!" Lily giggled. We piled into Alex's car and set off. As we approached Fort Canning, our headlights picked up a few parked cars and we felt gleeful. We parked and tried to see what was going on. We thought we saw a couple in the backseat of one car and another couple getting close over their steering wheel but our view wasn't great. Henry said he should have brought his bird-watching binoculars.

We stretched and craned our necks for a while and then Lily said *"Wah!"* as a police car pulled up next to us. The policeman got out of his car, rapped on our window, and barked something about "routine checking." He sternly told us we needed to leave. (He probably thought we were having some kind of orgy with all the people in the car.) As he left us, he started banging on the other cars. I thought to myself, 'Why do we have to leave? And why can't people just enjoy each other?' The whole situation made me feel rebellious. I felt Alex and I should have started hugging right on the pavement just to rattle the policeman, or at the very least we should have offered him a stick of banned gum.

Boat Quay

Before retiring for the night, I insisted on talking a quick stroll through Boat Quay, having heard about its festive setting. Alex explained that this area was once famous for its opium dens and sweatshops, but now feeds and quenches yuppies and tourists. In fact, we bumped into one of Lily's yuppie expat friends, a securities analyst. He came with us to Harry's, where Nick Leeson was once expelled for mooning his bottom. Then of course Nick ended up in far greater trouble, landing himself in Changi Prison.

Alas, I had to go to bed because my commercial shoot in Malaysia was the next day and I needed my proverbial 'beauty sleep.' Alex and Henry dropped Lily and I off back in Katong and I eagerly gave them big kisses and thanked them for showing me the spectacular sights of Singapore.

Off to Malaysia

Early the next morning, the alarm clock rang and Lily and I dragged ourselves out of bed. We hugged her mom good-bye and I thought happily about my brilliant tour through tropical urban life, of Peranakan culture, Singapore Slings, bird-lovers, and fabulous feasting.

Malaysian Outback

Arrival in Johor Bahru, Malaysia, via causeway,
April 29th

Selamat datang! Welcome to a Malaysian adventure. Lily and I headed off for a road trip into the Malaysian outback (we did plan to hit Kuala Lumpur as well), and the joy of the open road was thrilling. We were wild and free and venturing into the unknown. Lily said she has been coming to Malaysia since she was a child and it is a favorite destination for vacationing Singaporeans. I told Lily that my images of Malaysia were very much imbedded in the colonial age — sultans lounging in golden palaces, plantation owners sipping tonic water, pirate ships plundering through the Straits of Malacca, and tigers and head-hunters roaming the dense jungles. Lily grinned and said that it's a *little* different these days, although it is still a lush and mysterious land, filled with mountains, rivers, and rainforests. She said that much of peninsular Malaysia remains completely untouched, particularly the long mountainous region, Barisan Titiwangsa, running down the center from the Thai border to Kuala Lumpur. In the coastal areas, there are rubber and oil palm plantations, rice fields, and sleepy fishing villages. And she said that for hedonists like me, enchanting tropical islands are found along both coasts.

Commercial Shoot on Pulau Tioman

Our first stop was one of these enchanted islands, Pulau Tioman, where I would film the commercial. We reached Mersing, a port town on the east coast which is the jumping off point to over sixty different islands. Many of the islands conjure up images of great adventure with names like Pulau Babi Besar (island of big pigs) and Pulau Sibu (island of peril, known to have been the stomping ground of buccaneers). We hopped a boat to Tioman and sucked madly on fresh ginger to avoid getting too seasick on the two-hour ride. I told Lily that before this trip I had watched the 1950s Hollywood film *South Pacific* that was partly filmed on Tioman. I was looking forward to seeing the luscious scenery in person and frolicking around like the stars of *South Pacific* in my own little shoot. (Lily decided I needed to be spanked after that corny comment.) We reached Kampong Tekek, a small village on Tioman, and were met by Isaac, the producer from NYC, young and quite sexy in a professorial way. He whisked us to the launch waiting to take us to the shoot further south along the coast.

On the launch, we started discussing how commercials are a bizarre business because they are usually predicated on some kind of falsehood — a model says "I use this kind of shampoo and look how beautiful my hair is," or "I use this kind of toothpaste and look how white and shiny my teeth are." Isaac said that the model has probably never used the product, and the product is most likely not even used during the shoot. The hairstylist will use his/her favorite brand to style the model's hair, or the model's teeth will be painted white and smeared with vaseline for luster. I said that even if the spokesperson honestly does use the products he/she is endorsing, chances are it has nothing to do with the person's success. If Michael Jordan hadn't worn Nike sneakers, he would still have been able to make those dunk shots. We realized that if a product is being advertised you probably don't need it. If you did need it you would just buy it, and the company would not have to spend millions of dollars to demonstrate why you 'need' the product.

Regardless of the absurdity of the advertising business, I was there to shoot a commercial, and my job was to promote a product called *Supermodel Diet Coffee*. (Ugh! What a dumb name!) The pitch was that I drink this coffee and "it makes me super-slim and helps me to be a spectacular model." Especially after the previous conversation, I wanted to at least try the coffee before I shot the commercial. Unfortunately, living up to reality, Isaac said they didn't have it on the island. I started to feel very uncomfortable about being an integral part of this commercial's deception, and I asked Isaac to send the coffee to me in Kuala Lumpur, our next stop, so I could at least try it before the commercial aired. It still left my integrity way up in the air since I certainly wasn't drinking the coffee on a regular basis. I was beginning to have doubts as to how many more commercials I wanted to do.

When we landed on the shore I went right into the make-up trailer. The stylist gently chided me about my sun-burned face and unwashed hair and then got down to business working her magic. All made up in a flash, I hit the beach. Isaac gave me my lines and said that he wanted to film five or six different scenes. I took a few minutes to learn the first lines, repeating:

"Hi I am Jillian Shanebrook. Supermodel Diet Coffee helps me be the best model I can be! To be honest with you, coffee was never part of my daily routine because I really didn't like the taste, but with Supermodel Diet Coffee, I can't *stop* drinking it because it tastes so delicious ... I used to have to dump a dozen sugarcubes in my coffee so I could handle drinking it, but now with ..."

These lines were awful, and there was an inconsistency in the script: if I never drank coffee I certainly would not be putting sugar in it. I think the associate producer was too eager to play on the beach to take this script very seriously. I thought of a more consistent line and spruced up the language. As the lines needed to sound natural I had to 'get into character.' Since I actually don't like coffee (see how deceptive commercials are), I tried to muster some enthusiasm by thinking about *es jeruk* (fresh orange juice I drank in Indonesia). I am definitely going to lose my endorsement with all this talk, which is probably for the best.

We soon started filming. In one scene, Isaac directed me to lift arm weights to illustrate, according to the script, how 'strong and gorgeous' I was from drinking Supermodel Diet Coffee. Isaac needed several takes to get different angles, and my arms became so tired I could barely raise them for the last take. After a couple of hours the shoot was over. And despite the heavy weights I had to lift, the whole process was quite relaxing and it seemed ridiculous to have been paid so much. I still hadn't figured out why models are paid such outrageous salaries — I certainly hadn't yet done anything in my career that required much intelligence or any special skill.

On the way back to Kampong Tekek, Isaac told Lily and I that he had done a lot of research on Tioman before deciding to shoot there. He explained that because Tioman has been isolated from the mainland for hundreds of years, it has its own species of butterflies, cats, and plant life, completely unique to the island. Isaac said that there is one creature Tioman hopes to eliminate — the *crown-of-thorns starfish*. This starfish attaches itself to coral and ingests the coral's tissues, killing it within days. The only way to save the reef is to pry the starfish off, and then burn or bury them, as they can survive in the water for several months without any nourishment.

Once we landed at Kampong Tekek, Isaac and the crew were ready to debrief with everyone about the shoot and eat some barbecued shark at a nearby seafood restaurant. But Lily really wanted to get to Kuala Lumpur that night (we were going to stay with Lily's aunt) so we kissed Isaac and the crew good-bye, jumped a boat back to Mersing and were on our way.

Kuala Lumpur

Zooming towards Kuala Lumpur and bopping around to some 1970s Bee Gees music, Lily fascinated me with wild settler stories of Malaysia's capital city. Founded in 1857, Kuala Lumpur, or

KL as it is affectionately called, is a youngster amongst Asian metropoli. KL originally came into existence when 87 Chinese prospectors adventured up the Klang River looking to strike it rich. As the water became too shallow to go further, they stopped, and through the help of a *pawang* (magician) found deposits of tin. But these boys were in for some major trouble — in addition to tin, mosquitoes were abundant, and all but a dozen prospectors quickly died from an incurable fever (most likely malaria). The allure of fortune was too tempting, however, and a frontier town was soon born, filled with gambling lairs, opium dens, and 'houses of ill repute.'

Reaching KL in the middle of the night, we found our way to Lily's aunt's house and immediately crashed. The next day we slept in until noon. As we woke, Lily's cousin, Mira, bounded into our bedroom. Lily had said that Mira, at eighteen, was going through a 'rebellious' stage. And she did not disappoint — she was wearing dark black eyeliner, sporting a pierced nose, and had super baggy clothes. What is this I had read about Malaysian females — very soft, graceful, and passive? Lily said Mira was far from the typical Malaysian teenage girl — she was heavily into the sub-culture of grunge music.

Lily's aunt cooked us some *otak otak* (fish in coconut milk, wrapped in a banana leaf) and the Supermodel Diet Coffee sample arrived, so we had an eclectic lunch. Since I was becoming curious about Peranakan culture from staying with Lily's family, I asked Lily's aunt about their traditions. She sighed and said that for starters, old Peranakan weddings were much more exciting than weddings are today. She told us about the wedding of her grandmother, who grew up in Melaka. When her grandmother was of marrying age, a matchmaker studied the astrological signs of her and her potential suitors, whom her grandmother had never met, deciding if they were compatible. When a suitable husband was found, her grandmother was still not allowed to meet him. Then came her wedding — that lasted for ten days! There were all sorts of ceremonies, huge feasts, and presents, but even then her grandmother still could not see her husband. In fact, her grandmother was completely veiled for the entire ten days. Finally on the last day of the wedding, her grandmother led her husband to her bridal chamber, and during a ritual called *ching pang*, unveiled her face. After which, her husband said, "Miss, I have now to be rude with you" as was with tradition, and then they made love. Whether the groom was happy or not with his bride, or vice versa, the marriage had to be physically consecrated at once. My heavens. Sex with a complete stranger — and people think my generation is promiscuous.

After eating, we decided to get the feel for KL by walking around. This is a fairly intimidating task as the city is huge. The streets were teeming with people and before long we saw a 'medicine man' selling his oils and herbal concoctions on the sidewalk. He was smooth and fast-talking, showing off grisly 'before and after' photos of diseased body parts. Mira said these remedies are used for infections and even snake bites. Men also like to buy certain ones to increase their sexual prowess. Mercy! Between Singapore and Malaysia there is quite an obsession with stamina — there must be a lot of studly men in these parts. I ended up buying some to take home for some American men I knew, even though I thought they might be a bit offended. But hey, what are friends for? Beyond medicine for bedroom antics, the streets were full of snacks. There were Indian *roti* sellers serving hot bread with curry, *kachang putih* men, selling steamed peanuts and chick-peas, and my favorite — the *teh tarik* (pulled tea) men. This tea is made with milk and sugar and is cooled off by pouring the tea back and forth between two mugs — one mug held high over the head so the tea pours out like a waterfall. Mira said that she likes to watch because she always hopes that someone will miss and spill the tea. Mira was definitely into anarchy.

After the snack tour, Mira said, "I want to show you something cool *lah*" and we hopped on a *bas mini* (minibus), arriving at the Pudu Prison. Given Mira's rebellious stage, my first thought was that we were going to visit her current boyfriend in jail. But as we moved closer, it turned out she wanted to show us a brilliantly colored tropical landscape painted along the walls of the prison. Mira said that the mural was painted by the prisoners and is reputedly the longest in the world.

KL Nightlife — The Grunge Scene

Tired from the heat, we cooled off under the shade of a nearby palm tree by sucking on *chendol* (a dessert of shaved ice with red beans and gingko nuts). As evening set in, Mira started to get very enthusiastic about going to see an underground grunge band, and she begged us to go with her. Lily and I had planned to see a performance of *silat*, but I could tell that this girl was going to literally 'kick our butts' if we refused. We set out with Mira and eventually found the club, located in a nearly-hidden basement. As we entered, we saw a band of young boys who looked like they never combed their hair and had really unpleasant body odor. But with their raw, heavy jamming, reminiscent of Nirvana, I was duly impressed with the grunge skills this side of the Pacific. We weaved our way through the crowd towards the front and started dancing.

After an hour of dodging elbows and writhing bodies, I found a pocket of safety and watched Mira and Lily continue to slam-dance in the mosh pit. Of course a girl alone by the bar is like a water fountain in the desert, and a hunky Malay guy soon sidled up to me. He hit on me. "Where are you from?" I obliged, "From New York City." And I asked him where he was from.

"I grew up near Pekan on the east coast in a kampong."

"How do you like life in the fast lane in KL?"

He laughed and said, "Yes, it's okay. I've definitely joined the race of *boomtown bumiputras* (slang for Malay yuppies). My friends and I work long hours during the week here, but we usually head back to the kampong on the weekends."

"I know what you mean. I try to escape New York whenever I can … What's life like in your kampong?"

He sighed and said, "Well life is slower. One of my favorite times is around dusk when the air is cooling off and there is a delicious spicy smell of chilies cooking. I like to just walk around taking it all in."

He was so sincere and I was touched by his love for his village. I grabbed his hand and we rejoined the girls in the mosh pit, and sweet as he was, he head-banged like a champ. Many hours later, we girls ended up in a trance-like exhaustion back at Mira's house. We reeked of smoke and guys' smelly arm pits.

Back on the Road

The next morning we had a leisurely breakfast with Lily's aunt, and she packed us some *nasi lemak* (rice, sambal, and peanuts in a large leaf). She said this meal used to be taken on jungle expeditions. Then Lily shooed me into the car and I was surprised to see Mira in the back seat. Mira had not planned on coming with us but she said her father had grounded her for coming back late last night so she was 'out of there.' This girl was so *nakal* (naughty).

We headed north and soon passed by the Batu Caves — gigantic caverns which house a Hindu shrine. The caves, like the Sri Perumal Temple in Singapore, are a very popular site for the celebration of the Thaipusam Festival. Lily and I looked at each other and shivered thinking about sticking metal rods through our cheeks. Mira on the other hand, with her pierced nose to her credit, seemed perfectly calm. A little later, Mira said that we were about to pass by her dad's rubber plantation and I begged Lily to stop — I was very curious to see real rubber trees and the process by which latex is extracted from them. I found it amazing that products such as tires and rubber bands, which I had always thought of as inorganic, actually originate from the extracts of trees. Mira agreed but said we had to avoid her dad since she was supposed to be at home.

We drove in and found Rastam, one of the foremen. He was very kind and brought us out to the rubber plantation. He said that the Chinese started rubber tree tapping when they came to work in the tin mines in the late nineteenth century. The rubber trees looked like normal trees with sturdy grayish-brown trunks and pale green leaves. Rastam made a diagonal cut on the bark near the base of one tree and a white liquid started to drip out of the tree. Rastam said the liquid is latex and the best time to harvest it is in the early hours of the morning, before the heat stops the latex from rising. The latex is collected with a tin can and after several hours a small puddle will form. Rastam said this is not a very efficient collection method but is still the most commonly used. Once collected, acid is mixed with the latex, so that it can congeal and be sectioned and flattened into large sheets. These rubber sheets are then further processed and eventually exported all over the world. He said that Malaysia produces about 40% of the world's rubber. I couldn't help but think that a lot of this ends up as tires and condoms. Nice to know where it all comes from.

Rastam said that rubber tapping may look easy but it definitely has its occupational hazards. He said that in 1995, a rubber tapper near KL was found in the process of being swallowed by a reticulated python seven meters in length. The python was shot but the man's skull had already been crushed. It was presumed that he was dozing when the snake attacked and had been hopelessly trapped within the serpent's mighty body (weighing in at 140 kilograms). Hearing this, Lily squealed *"Wah!"* and before Rastam finished his story, we were already heading towards the car.

Before we drove off, Rastam gave us some *chempedak*, a fleshy, juicy fruit from the same family as jackfruit. Munching on the fruit, I quizzed little Mira about her lovelife. She said she had been dating a guy from The Malay College, a premier prep school for boys, who introduced her to the grunge scene. Mira said she was having second thoughts though, he just wasn't quite cool enough for her.

The Hill Stations

We were driving towards the central highland hill stations, up in the Barisan Titiwangsa range. The hill stations were originally built by the British in the early 1900s as an escape from the sweltering heat of the lowlands. And after sweating it out in KL, we were all thankful to the foresight of the English and thrilled to cool off 1,500 meters above sea level. We drove through spectacular green up to the Cameron Highlands, the largest hill station. Lily pulled off the road at one point and showed us a couple of small thatched huts of bamboo and palm leaves built on a steep slope. She said these were home to the *orang asli* (native people) who live today largely as they have for centuries, hunting with their blowpipes and poisonous darts, and often selling the bounty of the forest on the roadside.

We reached Ye Olde Smokehouse in Cameron and I felt like I was in the English countryside, in Devon or Cornwall. The house was a veritable English cottage in the Tudor style, its walls covered with ivy, surrounded by hollyhocks and English roses. Inside, there was a crackling fire in the hearth, and roast beef and Devonshire tea for supper. It was difficult to believe we were in Malaysia. As afternoon turned to evening, we sat on the verandah sipping tea, eating strawberry jam on toast, and watched a very gentile crowd head out for bird-watching and horse-back riding. Before long, the evening mist crept down and blanketed the mountains.

When it became dark, we three were ravenous and headed into the dining room. We were seated near a dapper tweed-wearing gentleman dining alone, and before long he had sent us over a bottle of Château Marjosse wine from Bordeaux. He soon sat down beside us, lit a cigar and started recounting his life story. His name was Harold Worthington, he was British and now working in KL in his own import/export business. He grew up in the African Sudan and was completely supporting his parents since their pension in Sudanese monetary pounds had gone to 'bloody hell.' London was 'for the wankers' but Malaysia was 'a smashing good time.' He was an avid bird-watcher and had been a contestant in the nearby Fraser's Hill International Bird Race last June, but twisted his ankle chasing after what he thought was a rare, crested fireback pheasant. He was a funny character and when he finished his third cigar he politely stood up, and, with a snappy 'Cheers,' exited the dining room.

Ghosts

The three of us giggled all the way up to our room saying, "That was a smashing good time," and "You're such a wanker." We took turns taking warm bubble baths and then all jumped into the one big bed together. I thought Mira would not stand for all this coziness, but she rested her head on my shoulder and fell asleep. It was so peaceful cuddling together under a blanket (I hadn't needed one in months) as a cool breeze fluttered through our open window.

A restful night however it would not be ... In the early morning hours we heard a woman's bloodcurdling scream and the words *"hantu, hantu!"* I sat straight up in bed, my heart pounding. Lily and Mira quickly started chattering in Mandarin and I asked them what was going on. With eyes wide opened, Lily said "Hantu means ghost!" Yikes! We ran down into the sitting room where one of the *amahs* (maids) was screaming and shaking. Nearby, several other amahs were also trembling. Harold Worthington soon appeared as well, murmuring that he was "knackered" (sleepy). Lily and Mira translated for me what the terrified amah, Fatimah, was saying. She had been sleeping soundly in her room when she woke up because she heard tapping at her window. She dove under her blankets horrified but the tapping continued. She finally peeked out and saw by the moonlight a man staring at her. But not just any man — a blue man! She immediately started screeching and quoting holy lines from the *Qoran*. Oh my.

Mira smirked at the whole situation and said "Malaysians are so superstitious *lah*!" She said she had been hearing about blue men since she was a little girl and Fatimah probably heard the same stories, and just thought she saw one. Mira rattled off a long list of Malay folklore she acquired from her grandmother: if you see a blue man you are supposed to throw water behind your back; if a person is possessed by an evil spirit, black peppercorns must be placed between the victim's toes and the *Qursi* (a holy Islamic verse) must be recited. If a women is pregnant, a pineapple must be buried under the house so the prickly thorns can deter the attentions of a particularly foul ghost who likes to make appearances with its intestines spilling out in full bloody glory. If you want to ensure sunny weather, you must call in a *bomoh* (witch doctor). Mira laughed and said that actually the bomohs could be legitimate. Her dad had told her about a group of actors in KL who ordered the services of a bomoh to ensure they had clear weather for an outside performance. The only night it rained was during an extra performance — the one night that wasn't covered in the contract.

Harold, however, exclaimed "Bullocks!" to Mira's skeptical monologue and said that Malaysians were not just being superstitious but were in fact taking necessary precautions in these mystical lands. He said not long ago he visited the nearby Genting Highlands, and one night over dinner a man told him a haunting story. Along the nearby Karak Highway, a married couple had been driving when they ran out of gas. The man went out for help, leaving the woman alone in the car. Soon after her husband left, the woman started hearing a thumping noise outside the car, but thinking it was just the wind, she turned up the radio. An hour later, her husband still had not returned with the gasoline. Worried, the woman decided to get out and search for her husband. As she stepped out of the car, she saw to her horror that a *pontianak* (female vampire) was banging her husband's head against their car roof!

Harold also said that not too far from here is *Tasik Cini,* a series of lakes which the orang asli believe to be home to a giant serpent with a huge undulating body that likes to tip over boats and devour fishermen. And he said not to forget about the legend of the *orang minyak* (oily man) who is black as night and runs around naked, lathered in oil. His mission is to rape female virgins in order to progress along the path of black magic. Well, at least we don't have to worry about the *orang utan.*

Fatimah was drinking some tea and seemed to have calmed down, but Lily and I were just starting to get panicky. I wasn't sure if Harold was trying to scare us even more so that we would invite him into our room for some cuddling under the blankets. Whatever his intent, we did all end up sleeping in the same room but not quite 'together' — Harold was stationed on a cot near the window to guard against any peeping blue men. We all fell back asleep hearing him grumble "Bugger it" as he tried to get comfortable on his narrow bed.

Strawberries and Butterflies

The next morning was in sharp contrast to the night before. Instead of worrying about orang minyak, we started the day off with a peaceful walk through some nearby strawberry fields. We greedily sampled the plump and juicy strawberries and quickly acquired red lips and tongues. We then visited a butterfly farm, marveling at butterflies in shades of ivory, scarlet, and copper, dappled with speckles of gold and green. They were darting among plants, stopping to sip nectar through their long thread-thin tongues that act like straws. We learned that butterfly life spans are sadly quite short — they usually live only two to four weeks.

We also visited the nearby Boh Tea Estate and gazed over acres of gorgeous emerald green tea plants, all shaped like level table tops. A guide told us that the plants are carefully pruned flat and short so the leaves can be harvested more efficiently — if left to grow naturally, the plants would be tall and skinny. The plants are very hardy, capable of producing tea leaves for over one hundred years. Having seen where rubber and tea come from, and the care in which they are harvested, I knew I would have much greater appreciation the next time I had a cup of tea or put on rubber galoshes.

Later that morning, we took a charming walk through a trail starting near Ye Old Smokehouse. We passed through pine trees and eucalyptus plantations and I thought for sure we would see a wood nymph or leprechaun spring out among all the lush moss, lichen, tree ferns, and orchids. We saw the famous pitcher plant (called *periuk kera* in Malay — literally 'monkey cups') which is among the few carnivorous plants in the world. It is very clever in that it secretes two fluids, one that is sweet and sticky to attract insects, and another which accumulates on the bottom of the 'pitcher' to digest the insects once they are trapped inside. Lily said that if we were quiet we might also see a *siamang* (a member of the gibbon family, the smallest and lightest of the apes). Lily said that siamangs live in complete monogamy and are petrified of water. To drink, they usually cling to a branch overhanging a river, dangle upside down, and rapidly dip their hand in the water, scooping some up. In addition to hydrophobia, they must also be scared of chattering young women because we didn't see any of them.

The Beach, Cherating

It was now time to hit the beach. Mira had been trying on some of my swimsuits and was begging Lily and I to take her to the ocean. (She said she wanted a chance to wear a bikini before returning home to her 'boring' one-piece suit.) We crossed over the spine of the peninsula and made it back to the east coast, to Cherating, home of Asia's first Club Med, but really just a lazy beach paradise of golden sand and thatched-roof bungalows.

Mira said we had to stay at a spot she had heard about called The Shadow of Moon at Half Past 4. Driving in, the ambiance did seem to be just about her speed — it was already dark, and the road was lit by torches in the shape of witches. Creepy. Inside, the baroque decor was dominated by animal bones, gnarled and twisted furniture, with red lanterns casting an ominous, bloody glow. This place seemed haunted and it looked like we were going to have another frightful night. I thought we should at least try to find some peppercorns for a possible exorcism.

Mira and Lily did not seem too scared and they ended up going to the hotel's nightclub, the Pop Inn, which had a reputation for serious dancing and flirting. I decided to turn in early because I was sleepy from all the fright the night before. I thought I would just peek into the nearby Dead Nightshade, known as 'the restaurant at the end of the universe.' As I peered in, a group of Malay boys saw me and immediately chimed in unison "Hello!" I had to go over to chat with them because they were so friendly. They worked at the restaurant, and before long Ahmad (the most talkative one) said, "Can *ah* take you for a walk?" Having picked up a little Malay English, I replied, "Can *lah*!" As we left, his friends were teasing, "Invite me *lah*!"

Coconuts, Chickens, and a Charming Man

Once we stepped outside, Ahmad asked me to wait and he disappeared around the corner; he soon returned holding the hand of a small monkey. Ahmad said the little guy was his pet and motioned for me to shake hands with the tiny primate. Once we were formally introduced, the three of us took a stroll along the beach. With a little prodding from Ahmad, his clever monkey climbed up a palm tree and a storm of coconuts rained down. Ahmad quickly took out a pocket-knife, slit the tops of the nuts, and soon we were sipping on fresh coconut juice. As we filled our bellies, I asked Ahmad about the period of emptied bellies and spiritual fulfillment, *Ramadhan,* and whether it was difficult to fast. He said that fasting is not a problem for him, but Ramadhan is hard on his mother because she has to rise very early to cook his family's breakfast which must be eaten before sun-up. He said Ramadhan always ends with the sighting of the full moon, and in his village when he was young, he had to help his father slaughter their chickens for the feast of Hari Raya (held on the day following the full moon). He thought of the chickens as pets and was heartbroken to kill them so he always prayed for a miracle. A few times, as his father was getting his ax ready, the full moon did not quite bloom, and Ahmad felt his prayers were answered since his little friends were safe for one more day.

All of a sudden, I wasn't sure what was happening, but with Ahmad's strong supple arms, bronzed skin, and thick wavy hair, he looked completely dreamy in the moonlight. He was saying something about fireflies — when he was young he used to collect them to put in bottles which they used like flashlights, and fishermen would search for them coming in at night, blah, blah, blah ... I couldn't concentrate on his words because he was so charming ...

A Swim and a Departure

The next morning Lily, Mira, and I woke ourselves up with a few cups of leftover Supermodel Diet Coffee (it was beginning to grow on us) and compared notes. They had danced most of the night with two Singaporean guys and I had spent some time on the beach with a man and his monkey. Mira got dressed, putting on one of my barely-there bikinis from the Supermodel Diet Coffee shoot. No wonder she wanted to get to the beach, she was bedazzling underneath all her baggy clothes. We went for a swim and after a few hours decided that we really needed to head back soon so that Mira wouldn't be disowned for disobeying her father.

So, we piled in to return to KL, and then to Singapore. I didn't want our adventure of grunge bands, rubber trees, blue men, strawberries, and smiling, friendly Malaysian people to end. Lily and I vowed to return in the near future to explore Sabah and Sarawak.

New York City Nightlife

Arrival at JFK Airport, New York, May 10th

I love Singapore. Kuala Lumpur is kicking and Jakarta, jumping. But New York City is still the place where the heart thumps a little faster. Even though I was a bit 'traveled out' from my adventures in Singapore and Malaysia, I was getting homesick. So I flew back home for a couple of weeks. It was a relief to return to my usual surroundings and persona, to be completely anonymous and just me — not a model.

7:04 pm, The Metropolitan Museum of Art,
Upper East Side

One warm evening, I headed out with two of my NYC friends — Katerina, a film maker, and Nathan, a Wall Street broker — to see what kind of mischievous excitement we could find. For the early evening, action is uptown; but for the late night you had better go downtown ... Our first stop was the Metropolitan Museum of Art — one of the finest art museums in the world. The young playboys and playgirls of the city gather here early on weekend nights to enjoy the rooftop garden on the third floor overlooking Central Park. This evening, the crowd sipped Chardonnay wine and nibbled on Brie cheese. Katerina and I observed and giggled as we identified three distinct New York types: *struggling artists*, dressed completely in black — the women with pale eggshell faces and brilliant ruby red lipstick (looking almost like geisha) and the men puffing on thin artsy cigarettes with the practiced look of boredom on their faces; Wall Street *power brokers*, still holding their business newspapers from the early morning; and *socialites*, whose day consists of rising at 11 am, having a power workout at the health club, late lunch at The Four Seasons, and shopping at Tiffany's. Everyone was looking at everyone else but pretending not to.

Studying the crowd, Katerina and I decided that the desired look in New York is Lean, Long-limbed, and Luscious (as well as Flawless, Photogenic, and Fabulous — not too different from my stylish friends in Singapore). Some people in New York actually think maintaining this appearance is more vital than food or shelter and end up spending all of their money on clothes and gym memberships. Katerina and I have a few acquaintances who look like movie stars and supermodels yet can't afford their own apartments. In brilliant acts of capitalizing on their inherent 'fabulous-ness,' they simply reside in pent-house apartments of the wealthy who welcome the 'ornaments' (in New York it's called *housedecoration*).

8:28 pm, Merchant's, East Mid-town

Our next stop was Merchant's, a yuppie bar in mid-town Manhattan. This is where yuppies search for their mates, particularly the males. For many New York men, their object is to find the finest looking, most accomplished, best-connected woman, sometimes referred to as a 'trophy' (which gives us some insight on these guys' feminist IQ). Nathan calls his older brother, a Wall Street millionaire, a 'hunter' because he is always hunting for the ideal female, dating a different überwoman each night of the week. New York is often about looking for something 'better.' The setting in Merchant's is certainly right for finding romance: dark

red velvet couches, flickering candlelight, and soft-spoken voluptuous hostesses. Katerina and I sat down and snuggled on a couch
while Nathan tried to get the phone numbers of models. We could
hear a lot of chatter about certain models visiting the 'spa'
(a euphemism for drug rehab programs). We also overheard one
poor young thing scream over her cell phone, "I don't care about
the fifteen grand! I'm not going to do the shoot for Clairol and
have my hair dyed yet another color! I need to stay blonde for a
few days!" She then collapsed into sobbing. I wondered if this was
where I was heading. I hoped not. Nathan eventually returned
with a fistful of phone, beeper, and cell numbers scribbled on
cocktail napkins. He was getting antsy to move on downtown, but
Katerina said she first had to at least make an appearance at an
MTV Party. (She had recently shot a 'Rolling Stones Rockumentary'
for them.) So we moved on ...

9:31 pm, MTV Party at Blossom's, West Mid-town

The party was held in what is a very exclusive florist shop by day.
So the setting was a tropical garden, with big, bright azaleas and
wisteria dripping flower fragrance in the air, bubbling waterfalls
and fountains, and even chirping green and turquoise parrots. I
felt like we had been transported to the jungles of the South
Pacific. There were also 'island girls' in grass skirts and coconut-
shell bikini tops who offered cigars, candies, and party toys like
massage oil. Katerina and Nathan got down to business working
the room *mwah-mwahing* with all the top execs and MTV celebrities. (Mwah-mwahing means speaking in a very complimentary
way. For instance telling a famous model that her new shoulder-
length bob looks 'mah-ve-lous,' even if you truthfully think it
looks matronly.)

I chatted with a director who insisted on getting my phone
number for an independent feature film he was shooting in a few
months. (The exact same exchange happens daily. The story is
probably true only about 10% of the time. Other than that, this is
the most overused pick-up line employed by amorous NYC males.)

Frankly we only had a 90-second talk sandwiched in between his cell phone conversations. Watching the antics of the party-goers was more rewarding — herds of models-in-training were talking up the male MTV personalities in their baggy surfer pants and baby pacifiers; entertainment TV reporters roamed the room interviewing anyone who looked important. They were going at such a pace that I thought they might mwah-mwah themselves to death. And their camera crews were covertly devouring the amazing feast (the food looked more like art) that was laid out — Cretan olives, *maki sushi*, Sicilian *antipasti*. Everyone else though had social-climbing, not snacking, on their minds. In the rush to get to the next MTV 'star,' chitchat seemed to last the length of a supermodel's mini-skirt.

Nathan and I eventually felt the need to escape, feeling slightly nauseous with the intense 'stargazing' scene. We grabbed Katerina, jumped into a cab and zoomed south.

11:27 pm, Cab, Mid-town to Downtown

The whole journey downtown in the cab Nathan, Katerina, and I were discussing the facts of the club scene. (As NYC traffic can be as bad as Bangkok's, it was a long ride and a long talk.) New York's nightlife is the model for nightlife around the U.S.A. and often the world — the fads and the fun start here and will eventually make an appearance in your own metropolis. Nathan said that clubs come and clubs go, usually lasting only two to four years due to the fickle tastes of NY clubbers. (Again, New Yorkers looking for something better.) One club, Area, redecorated its interior every month to avoid becoming passé, but it too was unable to survive and closed within a few years. According to Nathan, certain death for a club comes with the arrival of the 'wrong people.' Among the 'wrong people' are the *Bridge and Tunnelers (B&Ts)*, people who live outside the island of Manhattan and use a bridge or tunnel to get in. The street 'wisdom' is that this group is exceedingly 'unhip' and 'unmoneyed' and so destroys the 'cool' club atmosphere. You can certainly still be considered 'wrong' even if you live in Manhattan and are 'successful' (this usually means affluent): geeky investment bankers get turned away by the hordes every night. We agreed that the whole system is fairly ridiculous and simply a way for social climbers to construct exclusivity and a feeling of superiority. This is a side of New York that I really don't like.

Yet if you insist on becoming a truly 'hip clubber' (and once you are 'in,' it can be a lot of fun), Nathan, Katerina and I reveal these 'rules':

- Don't set foot in a club before midnight and refrain from complaining about the scene starting too late. You will immediately reveal that you are too old, have a corporate job, and are not tapped into the ways of *la vida loca*.
- Don't showcase your lack of club 'smarts' by heading right for the bar. Let someone else buy you a drink. This way people will think you are too 'important' to buy your own drink.
- And for goodness sakes, don't go *slumming* (going to a club beneath your social status) — if club promoters see you at the 'wrong' clubs, you won't be able to get into the 'right' ones.

Yes, these 'rules' are pretty inane.

Midnight, Webster Hall, East Greenwich Village

Arriving at Webster Hall, one of the most courted and heavily-trafficked nightclubs in the village, the crowds were moving into position for entry beyond the red velvet rope. Admission is by one of two methods. You are either on 'the list' — a list of names of friends of the club, including celebrities, rock stars, and models — and are automatically admitted; OR you are appraised as cool/sexy/good-looking enough to get in by your appearance alone. In general, it is much harder for a man to get into a club than a woman. One man trying to get in was particularly persistent. The doorman countered, "Your name is not on the list." Then the man tried three or four different names, "It must be under Jonathan, or maybe my middle name, Patrick, or my nickname, Rick ..." It was a sad and rather pathetic display. Then we watched the doorman approach an elegant young woman (who also wasn't on 'the list') and purr, "Right this way, darling ..." Since we knew the club owner, we walked right in. I couldn't help but think how silly the whole game was.

We immediately headed for the basement dance floor, descending stairs lit by candles. There was slow seductive funk music; bosomy females moved around the large room like slinky cats, males following them as if in heat. Couples danced so close to each other they appeared to be one body. The music was intoxicating and the dance floor started to look like a private bedroom. While Nathan went to the bar to get a drink, Katerina and I started dancing together. Before we got into the groove, a handsome man gingerly approached us and asked us both to dance. He said his name was Leon and that he was an actor in Hong Kong. We wanted to make him feel welcomed in New York, so we sandwiched him between us to enjoy two New York women. We had to say *"Joi kin"* though, as Nathan returned and shooed us up to the first floor.

Here, we found a huge vaulted space filled with writhing bodies and loud music — a modern-day cathedral of sweat and self-expression. We immediately spotted several transvestites (one of whom looked just like the famous Singapore drag-queen — Kumar) as well as a woman wearing nothing but an intricate painting on her chest. On one of the platforms sprinkled around the room, a muscular African-American man danced wearing only a black hood and a red sock around his 'protuberance.' On another platform a woman in a purple bikini and thigh-high leather boots was slowly gyrating her hips and running her fingers up and down her naked belly, showing us all how to really dance. Katerina and I couldn't stop laughing as Nathan stripped off his shirt (revealing a very toned chest, especially surprising for a businessman) and danced round the purple bikini woman. As the night continued, hundreds of red balloons fell from the ceiling, firecrackers went off, and all of a sudden I felt like we were in Singapore celebrating the Chinese Lunar New Year.

Finally, sweaty and exhausted, we were ready to try something different. I dialed the number of a naughty place I had wanted to visit for a while, and this is what I heard:

> *"Hello this is your mistress, you have reached La Nouvelle Justine's, an S&M fetish club … I know that you want to be spanked, slave, but you first must ask your mistress's permission. Disobedience of any kind will not be tolerated. I'm done now. Hang up the phone, slave."*

Then a meek male voice said: *"Yes Mistress."*

Well, because we were quite curious about an *S&M* ('pleasure from pain') club, we simply had to go.

1:58 am, La Nouvelle Justine's, Chelsea

La Nouvelle Justine's is found in Chelsea, a rather seedy part of New York City where the artist Andy Warhol, as well as the writers Dylan Thomas and Arthur Miller, used to dwell. Katerina giggled uncontrollably before entering La Nouvelle Justine's — Nathan and I had to promise her we would leave immediately if it was too weird. We boldly flung open the thick red door, first entering a small, darkened room, and then passing through heavy black curtains. The very first thing I saw was a man — naked, except for his underwear — with his Wall Street Brooks Brothers trousers around his ankles and his arms chained and hanging from the ceiling. His 'mistress,' who looked Japanese, was wearing a provocative *cheongsam*-like black dress, with a high neck and super-high slits up the sides so that you could see the slim outline of her buttocks whenever she bent over to spank him. Actually the technical S&M term is 'flog': the mistress held a whip, which looked like a black horse-tail, and she gently slapped the man's sensitive areas and then massaged him, moving her long red finger-nails between his legs front to back. The Wall Streeter writhed and moaned appreciatively, twisting his body around like a gasping fish. (Many businessmen and politicians seem to be attracted to S&M. Theory has it that people in positions of power like to be able to completely give up control — especially to a black-leathered dominatrix.) A second mistress soon stepped in, wearing fishnet stockings and high stiletto heels, her head shaven. Her instrument of pleasure was a long metallic wand that she gleefully used to tickle the victim's nipples. Continuous "oooohs" and "aaaahs" were heard from the chained man.

All of this happened while we waited for our young, blonde, shirtless host in tight leather pants to seat us — quite an introduction. On the way to our table, we also saw an adult-size highchair, a prison cell (I later learned you can request to be locked up and served only bread and water), old bizarre etchings of naked people all over the walls, and (for a true cold S&M look) barbed wire hanging from the ceiling. We sat down and ravenously studied the menu which included desserts such as *La Chaussure Fetiche de Justine*, described as a dark chocolate stiletto filled with mousse and fresh raspberries. But the really interesting fares on the menu looked like this:

Special

It's legal, but it's not tender. Not responsible for marked or swollen property.

Spanking
Dinner Served as Infant's Fare in the Highchair
Doggy Obedience Training
Foot Worship
Spanking of a Slave
Public Humiliation
Dirty Talk

For the uninitiated, the above menu consists of, in order: having the buttocks flogged (like our Wall Street friend), being spoon-fed like a baby, wearing a collar and barking, kissing the feet of the mistress, flogging a 'slave' yourself, getting berated and spanked in front of the assembled audience, and conversing in an extremely kinky manner. The menu also instructed that paddles were available in the gift shop for 'punishing' wayward lovers.

A grinning man with multiple tattoos soon came over to our table, introduced himself as Dane, and asked if he could sit down. After a few minutes of small talk, he moved right in for the kill. Turning to Katerina and I, he asked, "So what are you ladies into?" Katerina jokingly replied, "Multiple guys," and I said, "Being chained to beds." We burst out laughing at our little charade, but Dane thought we were serious and looked intrigued. Then Katerina mentioned that she had done striptease for a short time in San Francisco. Her specialty was performing in lesbian bars, where enamored girls would tuck fivers into her panties. Poor Dane was getting all worked up. Speaking to Katerina, he said, "Well I really like to watch … What would it take to get you up there in those chains? How about I buy you a drink, to get you relaxed …" Katerina politely refused his provocative offer and he lost no time in turning his attention to others. Soon after, we watched him flirt with a curvaceous redhead whom he later flogged.

3:12 am, Cab, Downtown to Uptown

After an eyeful of flogging and a few drinks, Katerina, Nathan, and I jumped into a cab back to safe (if not quite as exciting) uptown Manhattan, images of chains and whips still dancing in our heads. Of course we did stop for a warm pretzel in Times Square, like true New Yorkers after a night on the town.

SELLING BANANAS FRESH FROM THE VINE.

MY STUDENTS AND I – I TAUGHT THEM ENGLISH, AND THEY, IN TURN, EDUCATED ME ABOUT INDONESIA.

AT HOME – MY BUNGALOW, MY MOTORCYCLE, AND ME.

BALI

HIBISCUS AND INCENSE OFFERINGS.

FISHERMEN RELAXING UNDER THE COCONUT TREES AFTER THE MORNING TRIP OUT TO SEA.

AN ELABORATE HINDU ALTAR WITH OFFERINGS IN KUTA, BALI.

SINGAPORE

BOAT QUAY – NOT JUST A PLACE FOR SAILORS. THE PRESENT BOAT QUAY COMES ALIVE AT NIGHT WITH ITS SHOPS, RESTAURANTS, AND SIDEWALK CAFES.

SKYLINE OF SHENTON WAY AS A BACKDROP TO BOAT QUAY AND THE SINGAPORE RIVER – A BLEND OF BOTH CONCRETE JUNGLE AND GARDEN CITY.

BUSTLING CHINATOWN: SIGHTS, SMELLS, AND SOUNDS TO STIMULATE YOUR SENSES.

MALAYSIA

IT'S BACK-BREAKING WORK PLUCKING TEA LEAVES.

KUALA LUMPUR'S TWIN TOWERS –
AN UNFORGETTABLE LANDMARK.

IN BETWEEN TAKES ON THE TROPICAL
ISLAND OF TIOMAN.

MINGLING AT THE MTV PARTY IN MIDTOWN.

FANCY GETTING WHIPPED WHILE YOU EAT?

La Nouvelle Justine

READY FOR A NIGHT OUT.

INDONESIA

SELO. A TRANQUIL VILLAGE HIDDEN AWAY ON MT. MERAPI, JAVA'S MOST ACTIVE AND DANGEROUS VOLCANO.

SELO VILLAGERS.

WITH THE CHILDREN OF SULAWESI.

FRENCH RIVIERA

THE BEACH AT CANNES. STRETCHING OUT ITS INVITING LAND TO HOLIDAY SEEKERS.

THE GRAND MONTE CARLO CASINO IN THE EARLY MORNING MONACO LIGHT.

A FIELD OF SUNFLOWERS.

JAMAICA

Indonesian Covergirl Life

Arrival at Yogyakarta Airport, Indonesia, May 30th

I was very happy to return to Indonesia and quite relieved to have escaped New York without being flogged. Within a few days of my arrival, I set off with Matt and Lusi to a resort in the Sulawesi jungle for a short vacation. Yes, I was getting a bit spoiled with all of these holidays.

Arrival at Palu Airport, Sulawesi, Indonesia, June 3rd

We first flew into Ujung Pandang, a booming seaport in the south of Sulawesi, and then chartered a small airplane towards Palu, in central-north Sulawesi, about a two-hour ride. As we flew over green mountainous terrain, the ground below showed absolutely no signs of human habitation; we knew we were going deep into the jungle. At the tiny Palu airport, we were picked up by the resort owner, Pak Eko, who drove us to his bungalows nestled in the midst of dense flora on the Sulawesi Sea. For the whole of the next week, we lived the good life. We had daily massages on the beach from Mbak Sari, Pak Eko's daughter, who despite her diminutive size brought a reign of terror to our backs, pounding away and showing no mercy. We snorkeled, played tennis, sun-bathed, and read in the sunshine. We took big yellow banana rides (riding on a huge float shaped like a banana pulled along by a boat) in the clear waters, played with little girls from a nearby village, and warmed ourselves by towering bonfires at night. And no matter where we were, at precisely four o'clock, a delicious afternoon tea was served to us, with *es jeruk* (orange juice) and freshly baked *pisang goreng* (banana fritters). I knew that this life of leisure was getting out of hand when I saw Mbak Sari rubbing Matt's toes with rose oil.

There was one brief experience however that made us realize it wasn't all fun and games in the jungle. In the dining lodge, we read a newspaper article about a young boy who had a very unfortunate walk in a nearby area. While making his way through the jungle, a boa constrictor had attacked him, killing him by constriction. Then, by dislocating its jaw, the boa swallowed the boy whole. The photograph accompanying the text showed the snake, nearly four meters long, with its belly cut open and the boy inside, his body slightly decomposed and in a most sickly green color. We felt so sad for the little guy (the boy, not the snake).

At night Mas Budi, our young chef, cooked Sulawesi specialties: *cumi cumi bakar*, barbecued squid, and yummy *milu siram*, a corn soup with coconut and lime. Mas Budi was particularly interested in Lusi's opinion of his dishes, always asking her if she liked the taste and if she wanted a second helping. (Before long they were spending their afternoon tea side by side, munching and nervously tittering in each other's company.) Mas Budi's masterpiece was a *Torajan* dish, *pa'piong*, a mix of pork, chicken, and leaf vegetables smoked over a low flame and eaten with black rice. Mas Budi knew Torajan cooking so well because he was from the Tanatoraja mountains, north of Ujung Pandang. The Torajans are famous for their traditional houses shaped like buffalo horns, with the roof rearing up at the front and the back. Mas Budi told us that in addition to tasty food and unusual architecture, the Torajans have interesting burial customs. When a person dies, there are usually two funerals, one immediately after death, and one after sufficient money has been raised to buy enough buffaloes and pigs for sacrificial rituals. The number of animals sacrificed depends on the person's social position. And as the Torajans believe that you can take wealth into your next life, the dead are usually buried with great treasures. In the past, these graves were frequently plundered. But nowadays, the dead, and their riches, are hidden away in secret caves.

Before we left Sulawesi, Mas Budi suggested that we travel with him up to Manado, the capital of North Sulawesi, where we could try *lawang pangang* (stewed bat), *rintek wuuk* (spicy dog meat), and *kawaok* (fried 'forest rat'). Love-struck Lusi thought that sounded fabulous. As for me — hmmm, I think not. In America these are not typical snacks to say the least ...

Arrival at Yogyakarta Airport, June 10th

Another Cover Story

Returning to Yogya, I found that *Matra Magazine*, another Indonesian men's magazine, had faxed me in my absence. They inquired if they would be able to send a couple of photographers to Yogya for a cover shoot to 'capture' me at home. I agreed, and a few days later Mas Driego, Matra's resident photographer, and Mas Heriyadi, a freelance photographer, arrived in Yogya. I met them at their hotel for a drink and we discussed our ideas for the cover. We decided on several shoots over the next few days — at my house, along the beach near Parangtritis (a coastal town south of Yogya), and in Mas Heriyadi's hotel room.

The next day, we were set to shoot in my lush garden where the ginger plants were blooming with brilliant ruby flowers. Mas Driego instructed me to make up my face to resemble a 'seductress,' with heavy eye-liner and full red lips. He said he wanted to shoot me in my own clothes to show my personal style. Because he was shooting for a men's magazine, he went through my wardrobe picking out the 'sensual' articles. (A task that wasn't too hard as my closet was filled with impractical items.) Wearing a silk strapless dress with my full make-up, I felt a bit ridiculous in front of my housekeepers, Mas Mujiran and Mbak Titi, who had never seen me looking like such a 'vamp.' They smiled at my appearance, but I felt like they must have thought I was very *nakal* (naughty). I could see them giggling with each other as they watched me pout for the camera all afternoon.

The following day we went to Parangtritis, where an angry sea goddess, Nyai Loro Kidul, is reputed to dwell. Many Indonesians believe she is attracted by the color green, and lures victims into the sea to drown them. The drownings are probably related to the fact that most Indonesians never learn to swim, but regardless, no one wears green on the beach. Mas Driego had me pose on the sand near some rock formations, shooting for nearly four hours while I became a bit exhausted holding difficult poses. One of these shots ended up on the cover and you may be able to make out a slightly pained expression on my face, as I held up my left arm in a very unnatural position. On the way back to Yogya, we drove through the stark isolated beach towns of *Kukup* and *Krakal* and I was hoping we wouldn't get a flat tire and be stranded there.

Our final shoot the next day was in Mas Heriyadi's hotel room, where he wanted me to pose in lingerie. It was strange to be alone with him in his hotel room while I was in a revealing brassiere and panties; although he was very polite I did sense some sexual tension. At one point while we were shooting, he asked me to remove my bra. He said he wanted to take an artistic nude photo, in which my body would be blurred, and the vase of flowers behind me would be the focus of the picture. (All of a sudden I found myself in a scene from a cheesy made-for-TV modeling movie: photographer tells model to take her top off.) Cheesy as it was, I was conflicted: his explanation was rather uninspiring, and I couldn't quite believe the premise. I was worried I would end up the focus of the photo and that this nude picture might somehow become public; something I wouldn't want happening especially as I was becoming more well known. Philosophically, I felt that there was nothing inherently wrong with posing nude — why should we hide our bodies? Yet realistically, I knew that the majority of society, particularly in conservative Muslim Indonesia, did not share my view. I was afraid that if this picture did become public, I would be branded as an immoral Westerner. Yet even though I did not want to take the picture, as a model I felt a great deal of pressure to follow the photographer's directions. After a long discussion — I explaining my misgivings, he explaining the artistic merits of the shot — I was eventually persuaded. It was a decision I almost immediately regretted, knowing that the use of the picture had now been taken completely out of my control. After the shot, I pleaded with him to keep the photo in his private collection and he agreed. But I still felt uneasy.

In hindsight, I realized I was new at modeling — insecure and gullible. As a photographer he held immense power, including access to a magazine cover; I acquiesced because I wanted to do a good job and be successful. This is a photographer/model dynamic that is continuously played out in the fashion world.

Night Intruder

Soon after, my second magazine cover appeared throughout the country, and it was not quite as much of an event for me as my first cover. The novelty of being splattered on every newsstand had worn off a bit. (Was I already becoming 'jaded'?) Yet my daily life was beginning to change. With two high-publicity magazine cover stories, I was becoming recognizable. For the first time I experienced what it is like to be famous and always on display. When I ventured outside, people would often stare and point at me, whispering to their companions and sometimes approaching me to ask for an autograph. I felt very frustrated because I wanted to interact with Indonesians and loved talking with people on the streets. Yet I was growing exhausted of being a curiosity. I started to go out less. Even if I ventured out, I wore an enormous sunhat, sunglasses, and baggy clothes as a bit of a disguise. The strain climaxed when I had an uninvited night visitor.

I woke up one night around three in the morning and felt confused. I wasn't thirsty, I didn't need the bathroom, I didn't hear any noises, but yet I was wide-awake. The longer I laid in my bed, the more I sensed something was amiss in my house. I noticed that my bedroom door was open and I was certain I had closed it before going to bed. I was about to get up to investigate when I saw a shadow move ominously towards the opened bedroom door, and then the darkened figure of a man surreptitiously entered my bedroom. I immediately sprang out of bed and started repeating in English, "Who are you?" I didn't feel scared at that point, just angry and curious who this man was. The man froze, then turned around and started running. I chased him through my study into the living room and through the kitchen, straining to catch a glimpse of his face. When he reached the kitchen door, he pushed it open, ran outside, and swiftly slammed it shut, holding it closed while I struggled to open it. Mas Mujiran, my housekeeper, heard the commotion and came running over. Seeing Mas Mujiran, the intruder let go of the door, sprinted across the backyard, and scaled a tall fence by leaping up a ladder that he must have left there for a quick escape. Poor Mas Mujiran sprained his ankle trying to follow him over the fence. Within fifteen minutes however, Mas Mujiran had assembled a band of neighborhood men, all carrying medieval-looking torches, to hunt him down. They searched through the night but were unable to find him. I was actually relieved because Mas Mujiran told me they would have killed him. I really did not want the man to die just because he became a bit obsessed.

What was especially eerie about the intrusion was that I usually locked the kitchen door at night, but I had returned home late that evening and had forgotten to lock it. It is likely that the intruder had been trying to enter for many nights before he was finally able to get in on that one night. The worst moment of the ordeal occurred while I was looking around the house to see if anything was missing. I noticed that in my study, dozens of my modeling pictures had been laid out on my desk, pictures that I kept in a drawer next to my bed in my bedroom. I realized that at some point before I woke up, he had been searching through my drawer next to my as I lay sleeping. Yikes! For months afterwards, I went to bed with my dressers against my bedroom door and felt terrified falling asleep. When I did finally drift off, I had the same recurring dream: on my way to the airport, returning to America, I got into a taxi, the doors promptly shut and locked, and then the taxi driver turned around, showing the darkened face of the intruder. There were no *mimpi indah* (sweet dreams) for quite a while. Yet there was one small consolation: at least the intruder hadn't been blue.

Arrival at Honolulu International Airport, Hawaii, July 25th

I needed a break from my new life as a 'celebrity,' particularly from stalkers. So I flew to Hawaii to see an old boyfriend, Rob, who was working as a scuba dive instructor on the little island of Lanai. Lanai was once the home of large pineapple plantations, and many residents are originally from the Philippines, recruited for pineapple picking. Tourists, not pineapples, now dominate Lanai. Hmmm, I think I would stick with the pineapples. The first night Rob took me out to Honolulu for a Hawaiian dinner of *mahi-mahi* (warm-water fish popular in Hawaii). I then suggested going to Waikiki Beach to see a *hula* dance performance. He agreed and for the rest of the evening we were transported back to old Hawaii, watching smiling hula girls in their grass skirts and flowered *lais* tell stories through the swish of their hips and the grace of their arms. Reflecting upon Hawaiian geography, their body movements described island features, such as the ocean, waves, dolphins, and reefs. I later did a hula dance of my own for Rob, describing my hometown, New York, using the 'grace of my arms' to convey the 'beauty' of gargantuan skyscrapers, honking taxi cabs, and belligerent supers!

Upon first look, the Hawaiian Islands with their tropical island culture seemed very similar to Indonesia. They didn't immediately feel like the United States. But with closer examination, I knew I was back in America: everyone spoke English, and I had all the conveniences of home, including American newspapers and the telephone. I relished being completely unknown and just relaxed, talking to my friends and family in New York for hours, tooling around the island in Rob's jeep, and nibbling on Hawaiian macadamia nuts.

Arrival at Mataram Airport, Lombok, Indonesia, August 2nd

Gili Islands

I was not quite ready to return to Yogya, so on my way back from Hawaii I stopped off to meet Matt on Lombok, an island just east of Bali. While travelling in Bali, we had heard about a group of tiny coral-fringed islands off the coast of Lombok that were a 'must-see.' Matt and I traveled from Mataram, the capital, to the northwest Lombok coast where we caught a little blue boat out across the Lombok Straits, heading for the Gili Islands: Trawangan, Meno, and Air. We decided on Gili Trawangan, the farthest island out, because it is known as the destination for superb snorkeling and sexy socializing. As soon as we arrived, we knew we were in a very lively place. We could see dozens of revelers splashing on the shore, tanned guys and girls paddling by in kayaks, little beach cafes, and not a single automobile or motorcycle to ruin the fantasy island atmosphere. The only mode of transportation was the horse cart, complete with bells. The bells reminded me of Christmas ("Jingle Bells"), but happily the tropical weather didn't. Matt and I rented a bungalow on the beach for the equivalent of a few dollars, and then as Matt was parched he went off for some Bintang Bir (Indonesia's home-brewed beer). I decided to go snorkeling and check out the fish.

I hopped into a little red bikini, put on my mask and fins, and walked out to the beach. As I dived into the azure waves, I entered a quiet world of pink and purple coral, and fish of spectacular shapes and colors. There were green parrotfish with intricate wavy patterns of lavender and blue, their hues resembling a Monet watercolor. Yellow polka-dotted boxfish with cubed bodies were floating around awkwardly, using only their pectoral fins and moving like tiny underwater helicopters. Blue tangs pursed their deep indigo rubbery lips as they floated by. I was mesmerized by the dazzling fish and shamelessly followed them around, wanting to be part of their world. As I trailed a yellow-striped angelfish, I came upon the hull of a large fishing boat. I did not want to swim around the boat as it was very long and the reef quickly dropped off into deep, dark waters (sharks had been sighted), so I popped up from the sea to walk along the beach.

Boy on the Beach

There upon the shore was an Adonis: muscled, sun-kissed, with lustrous white teeth, and jet-black curly hair down to his elbows. I immediately felt embarrassed because I had just taken off my snorkeling mask and I knew that I had a bright red imprint of the mask on my face. I was not looking my best, and I tried to back up into the water so I could let the redness settle down before talking to this heavenly creature. Too late. He saw me. We started to chat. He said his name was Marcos and he was from Colombia. He was traveling around Southeast Asia for a year with his brother and two cousins, and had just spent two months in India. I felt like a star-struck schoolgirl as I talked to him, hardly able to articulate my words because my brain was preoccupied with one thought, circulating like a flashing neon sign — 'He's so hot!' But I guess I made a decent impression on him as he invited me to a party that night at the local hang-out — The Excellent Bungalows.

I left the beach giddy with excitement and found that Matt had caught the attention of two Danish girls, Sabine and Annabell. Matt was 'keen' on going to the party, so that night we set out for The Excellent. Okay, I admit it. As soon as we arrived, I scanned the room for Marcos. He wasn't there yet, but most of the island's other visitors were — they were chatting about the day's activities, which included scuba diving among blue reef sharks, eating fresh lobster for lunch, and kayaking over to Gili Meno. Suddenly I saw Marcos walk in. He saw me, smiled, and my heart started thumping as I watched him walk over to me, kissing me on both cheeks. We talked for hours. Marcos was so flirtatious, excited, and energetic about everything, with exclamations like "Oh you live on Java, tell me all about it!" I loved listening to his luscious Spanish accent and his stories about Latin America. He told me that since his father is a wealthy businessman in Bogota, the Colombian mob had tried several times to kidnap him and his brother in order to extort money from his family. During one attempt, as Marcos was driving home at night, a jeep pulled up beside him and a man waving a machine-gun motioned for him to pull over. Marcos refused to pull over and instead accelerated. Soon the two vehicles were in a high-speed chase. The jeep tried repeatedly to force him off the road, so Marcos had to swerve wildly into the incoming traffic while dodging machine-gun bullets that were flying in through his windows. Miraculously, he made it safely into his family's compound. The next day, his father had bullet-proof windows installed in all of the family's cars. The whole tall, dark, and handsome thing, along with dodging bullets, was just too much. Yow-Za! I fell for him.

By the end of the night, guys were luring girls down to the beach to show them the tiny phosphorescent sea creatures that were lighting up the water. I could not resist Marcos' invitation, so I sat down on the sand with him in the soft moonlight where we could see thousands of stars. I also caught a glimpse of Sabine and Annabell throwing their bikini tops to the ground as they went skinny-dipping with Matt. His Aussie charm had obviously worked and I had a feeling the bungalow would be mine alone that night. Marcos started to get cuddly and asked if he could kiss me. I giggled and said yes ...

Over the next few days, Marcos and I played in the warm Eden of Gili Trawangan: I sat in his lap and admired the darling freckles on his nose, kissed his soft lips, took him kayaking, and he read me passages from the philosophers Nietzsche and Camus. His mind was sharp and compassionate, and every time I looked into his eyes, I felt like I had known him for a long time, and my heart swooned. Unfortunately, our time together was painfully short since Matt and I had to get back to Yogya.

The morning we had to leave, Matt and I both sadly packed up (he had fallen for Sabine ... and also Annabell) and headed to the tiny port. As the little blue boat was getting ready to sail for Lombok, I felt an overwhelming need to see Marcos one more time, so I frantically hopped on a horse cart to try to reach his bungalow. Matt nervously called after me to hurry back. After a few minutes I realized I couldn't make it in time, so I wrote Marcos a good-bye note and asked the driver to deliver it to him. I returned to the shore just in time to catch the boat. As we floated back to civilization, I started to cry. And soon I was sobbing. Matt put his arm around me as I gazed longingly back at the little island during the entire boat ride. It was such a magical paradise and my heart ached to leave it. I feared that I would never be able to truly experience the island again, particularly as development encroaches so rapidly on lovely places.

Arrival at Yogyakarta Airport, August 7th

Movie-Making

Although I was a bit depressed about my return to Yogya (I missed my 'Latin lover' and the anonymity of a tiny isolated island), my spirits were raised by some news. One of my students told me he was working as a production assistant on a historical film that was shooting nearby. He soon recruited Sophie and I, along with some European girls from Yogya, to play refined Dutch ladies.

On the day our scene was ready to be filmed, we drove north from Yogya for a few hours, arriving at an old Dutch colonial estate. After several hours of make-up and costume-fitting, we ended up spending the night waltzing around a huge ballroom for a prim party scene. Our partners were authentic, older Dutch men from Jakarta who had lived in Indonesia their entire lives. We had to do our scene dozens of times, because one of us, usually one of the men, would trip on a waltz step. The film aired on RCTI but I never saw it — my 'big film debut.' Matt saw the film and teased that he certainly could have whirled me around better than 'that Dutch fellow.' Hmmm ... perhaps a smidgen of jealousy?

Selo

After our screen debut, Sophie and I continued with our adventures. We decided to climb nearby *Gunung* (Mount) Merapi, one of Java's most active and dangerous volcanoes. We set off a few days later, riding my motorcycle up towards the mountain village of Selo, perched on the northern side of Gunung Merapi. Along the way, we had some engine trouble and had to walk my motorcycle a few kilometers to a roadside mechanic. The situation was a bit perplexing because I didn't know any Indonesian motorcycle vocabulary and was completely unable to explain what was wrong to the mechanic. He started puttering while we drank some tea and hoped for the best. A couple of hours later, the mechanic finished and smiled; we figured that was a universal sign for success. So we continued on, braving rain showers and winding roads so steep I thought the motorcycle was going to be pulled off the road by gravity. Finally, we gratefully arrived into the cool temperatures and mountain air of beautiful Selo. The scenery, the crispness of the air, and the rugged, hardy look of the people reminded me of Nepal — it was as if we had traveled to a corner of the Himalayas.

Accommodations in our hotel were simple but quaint. We walked around the village delighted by the sturdy, humble houses and tranquil lifestyle: women were sitting outside talking to each other, children were playing, and we even stumbled upon a performance of traditional Javanese dance. Villagers in colorful batik were dancing to gamelan music on a small plateau overlooking the town. In late afternoon, the sun added decoration to the scene, casting pink rays on the dancers. We tried to discreetly watch and not disturb, but before long, a young woman came over to us and motioned for us to join the dance. We held hands with the young and old, trying to mimic the steps, providing a lot of entertainment for the villagers as we couldn't quite catch on. Their kind gestures made us feel like part of the village that night.

After the dance, we went to bed early in preparation for our climb up Gunung Merapi. We rose at about one in the morning to begin our attack of the mountain, led by a guide we had hired, Mas Agus. At the back of our minds loomed the fact that Gunung Merapi had exploded just months earlier, killing 69 people. The mountain was still periodically rumbling, and climbing from the southern ridge was impossible at that time because of lava flows. Even the northern route that we were taking was 'officially' closed.

As we climbed, the night was thick with hardly any light from the moon or stars to illuminate our way. Our flashlights were difficult to carry because the mountain was steep and we were often on all fours, inching our way up. Mas Agus though, was like a mountain goat, always several steps ahead of us. He told us that he usually leads at least one tour up the mountain each night, sometimes (if his climbers are fast enough) he has time and energy to lead a second. After several hours, we reached the summit in time for the sunrise. The sky was clear for a spectacular view of the plains of Yogya. Mas Agus said we could climb over a ravine to see fireholes of molten lava, but because we could hear grumblings from that direction we thought we had pushed our luck far enough. As Sophie and I snapped pictures of ourselves to record our ascent, we joked with Mas Agus, "Today, Mt Merapi; Tomorrow, Mt Everest."

'Hitting the Big Leagues'

Soon after, I was voted one of the top two favorite covergirls in Indonesia (from my Popular and Matra covers), ahead of dozens of famous film stars, singers, and models. I was featured in calendars for Popular and Matra and started getting sacks of fan mail. (A very funny experience — I didn't exactly understand why people were writing to me.) Both magazines invited me to be a columnist and write about my life traveling and modeling.

It was time for me to join some modeling agencies. I soon signed with Carrie Models in Jakarta, Bess Models in Singapore (who would represent me throughout Asia) and Thompson Models in New York (who would represent me throughout the U.S. and Europe). With my upcoming international itinerary and full schedule, I would need a small crew to help me: my modeling agents would find me clients and endorsements, negotiating all my contracts; my booker would schedule my modeling jobs; and I hired a personal assistant to make all my travel arrangements, keep my finances organized, and take care of everyday tasks such as shopping and sending clothes out for dry-cleaning.

It was very strange to have all these people involved in my career, as if I were an 'important' person; I didn't feel important, but like just another 'attractive robot.' I quickly realized that my agents were 'important' — they were the ones behind the scenes who were the star-makers and breakers, holding all the access to clients and 'supermodel-dom.'

The French Riviera

Arrival at Charles De Gaulle Airport, Paris, France,
September 15th

After weeks of non-stop modeling, including runway shows in Jakarta, a commercial in the U.S., and a romance book cover, my agent sent me over to Paris for a French lingerie shoot. Afterwards, I took a luxurious vacation on the French Riviera, the Mediterranean Coast of France. The French Riviera is undoubtedly the favored glitzy playground of the lovely, moneyed, and famed. Riviera guests have always included the reigning queens and kings of the celebrity elite, from Brigitte Bardot (who was the first to sunbathe nude on the Riviera in the 1950s) to supermodels by the planeload, who descend upon the Riviera for doses of sun, sea, seduction, and frequently, scandal. This is where bronzed buttocks and bare breasts are as common as suntan oil. My older sister Kate (who flew over to meet me) and I discovered that the Riviera nightlife is even more sizzling than the sun-baked white sand.

5:00 pm, Pampelonne Beach, St. Tropez

After an afternoon of bikini shopping along the narrow cobblestone streets of St. Tropez, Kate (spunky, smart, and long on looks) suggested that we head towards the beach for some late afternoon sunning and flirting. St. Tropez is often called *St. Trop-d'Aise* (St. Too Much Luxury), since it is the preferred stomping ground of the 'Beautiful People' and the premier venue for parading buff bodies, from convertible Porsches to Spanish lovers. Reaching the beach, at first glance, everything looked normal, bronzed and graceful sunbathers strolled in their Versace sunglasses and lounged on their Saint Laurent beach mats, lathering on Bain de Soleil. But looking more closely, I couldn't quite believe my eyes: the bikini bottoms on the guys and girls were the tiniest I had ever seen, really just a few threads around their *derrières*. These tiny bottoms were so popular that there were bikini bottom vending machines all over the beach. Kate and I quickly popped in our French *francs*, scooted into a dressing room to change, and were soon parading the beach in little blue bottoms. Our sauntering led us to a sharp drop-off on the far western side of the beach where we watched brawny men and voluptuous women jump off the bank and float in the turquoise water. Kate and I took the plunge and the water felt cool and lovely around our bodies. To reach the beach again, everyone had to hoist themselves up the bank with a rope. Kate couldn't stop giggling as we watched a large group of men congregate on top of the bank, helping the women up the steep climb and getting a huge eyeful of their topless, wet ascent. More than once we noticed a helping hand turn into a watch-the-sunset-in-my-Ferrari invitation.

We settled down under two pastel-colored umbrellas and analyzed the interactions of the generic French Riviera beach dwellers — the local guys, the fashion models, and the rich businessmen. The local guys, identified by their sun-streaked hair and browned bodies, were flexing their muscles and hoping that their dark glasses would mask the fact that they were watching the girls; the models were pouting into their Chanel compact mirrors trying not to get sun-burned for their upcoming runway shows; and nearly every businessman had one hand on a cellular phone, making a business deal in Madrid or Hong Kong, with the other hand on the supple thigh of his sultry French girlfriend. The crowd also included sunbathers from neighboring Mediterranean climes, and Kate and I couldn't avoid the attention of two Greek shipping magnates. After sending over several fruit drinks, they tried to romance us with their French. I had to laugh as Nico kneeled before my sister and said, *"Tu es comme une tigresse"* (You are like a tiger), while his brother, Stavros, said to me, *"Je t'avale tout avec mes yeux"* (I swallow you completely with my eyes) and *"Tu brises mon coeur"* (You crush my heart). After much begging by the Greeks, we decided to accept their offer of a wild night cruise aboard their yacht for Cannes, Monaco, and Monte Carlo.

8:00 pm, Le Baboon, The Mediterranean Sea off of St. Tropez

Kate and I strolled through the St. Tropez harbor toward our Greek friends' yacht *Le Baboon* (Stavros later told Kate that the yacht was named in honor of Nico's rather furry body) admiring the boats of pleasure anchored in this port, commonly referred to as 'Millionaires' Row' by French locals. As we approached *Le Baboon* we could hear loud funk music and we realized we were not the only guests the Greeks had invited — at least twenty-five hipsters could be seen grooving on the upper deck. Once on board, Stavros introduced us to several Greek men, all cousins and friends of his and Nico's. Then he gave us a tour of his yacht, which he called a 'mega-yacht,' at thirty-four meters long with a crew of ten, including two masseuses. The yacht was opulent, decorated in seventeenth-century Italian decor, with Venetian furnishings, frescoed ceilings, and fragrant purple jacaranda flowers. Stavros led us into a large hall where the food and *Oezo* (licorice-flavored Greek alcohol, pronounced "OOzo" and strong like battery acid) were plenty. As the yacht sailed towards our first stop, Cannes, we all dined on lobster and mango soup, foie gras, and Beluga caviar. After dining, we followed the Greek custom of breaking the dinner plates, smashing them on the floor.

11:45 pm, Motorcycle, Cannes

Our yacht docked at Cannes just before midnight. Transportation was now via motorcycle, and Stavros invited me to ride on the back of his Harley Davidson, with Kate on the back of Nico's Suzuki. Soon we were all zooming to an exclusive Cannes disco. I felt like I was riding with Jackie Chan's Greek cousin as Stavros weaved in and out of traffic at a breath-speaking speed. I held on tightly and asked Stavros why he and his brother spent so much time in France, and not Greece. He quickly enlightened me with the facts of the French lifestyle.

He said he admired the French for three essential qualities: their women, their lifestyle, and their romantic philosophy. He said the French female is a woman *sans pareille* (without parallel). Her mannerisms, speech, and appearance are overwhelmingly sensuous, down to the last detail. For instance, she never leaves the house without a generous splattering of *parfum* on all her erogenous zones and sometimes flirtatiously wears her lover's undershorts instead of her own panties. "Ooh la la... *très* sexy," purred Stavros. As for lifestyle, the French are well-acquainted with indulgence — they drink the finest French wines, eat the best cheeses and breads, and, amidst such splendor, work as few hours as possible. And as for romance, Stavros explained that he and his brother's romantic practices are exquisitely compatible with the French, "*Conquérir, c'est bien, mais chasser, c'est magnifique!*" (To conquer is fine, but to hunt is magnificent!) The French are also delightfully obliging, in the event that a wife strays with an *amoureux* (lover) or a husband with a *maîtresse* (mistress), it is the custom to philosophize "*Ah, c'est la vie!*" (Stavros mentioned that as Nico is married, Nico truly appreciates this view.) Well, Stavros was probably not going to win any awards for spiritual enlightenment, but there was something amusingly innocent about he and his brother's pursuit of physical pleasures — they were quintessential 'boys.'

Midnight, Caves du Puy Disco, Cannes

We arrived miraculously in one piece at the middle of downtown Cannes. As we walked towards our destination, Stavros told us that discos are known as *boites de nuit* (night boxes) in France, and in Cannes they are packed with fresh-faced, frisky hedonists. Stavros said that Cannes is especially renown for "*très* chic" foam parties, in which revelers dance among soapy bubbles. It's a big booming bubble bath. He added that entrance into a Cannes nightclub demands one 'requirement' — stunning looks. As Cannes is one of the most glamorous Mediterranean ports, jet setters have been knocking down its nightclub doors for nearly a century and one faces stiff competition to get inside. If you arrive in May during the sexy Cannes International Film Festival, Stavros added, you had better be drop-dead devastating because you will have to compete with all the Hollywood film stars and agents who have loads of leverage. Nico warned that on the Riviera, it helps to be a night-owl because clubs open at midnight, closing only when the beaches warm up in the morning. As far as being hip to the scene, Stavros and Nico, our Riviera playboys, were very helpful accessories. I will have to return the favor when they visit New York. And even though the Riviera shared all the pretentiousness of New York nightlife, the scene was somehow a bit more charming because it was foreign and the 'rules' could be rationalized as amusing customs of the French. (But who needs these customs at home?)

When we reached our destination, Kate and I followed Stavros into the Hotel Byblos, and then through the private entrance of the Caves du Puy, a slick club with an ambiance inspired by Egypt. A cocktail hostess dressed like Cleopatra handed us some pink champagne and I could see dozens of the elegantly-attired lounging on saffron sofas shaped like camels, showing off their Riviera tans. We too reclined on the couches drinking our champagne and were soon joined by Monique, a bosomy blonde, who had briefly been Nico's lover. Kate and I chatted with Monique, and when Kate told her that I lived in Asia, she said that French women are obsessed with Asian men. Tony Leung Kar Fai was recently voted *the* Asian man whom French women would most like to get to know intimately.

Later on, Monique invited Kate and I to dance. She led us up to a stage in the middle of the room. And all eyes were on us as we intertwined our legs and moved our hips to the Euro dance music. Stavros and Nico glanced up at our steamy stage spectacle, looking a little jealous as we were clearly enjoying the company of our new friend. Before long, Monique removed her black bra, flung it out into the crowd, and started to reach for Kate's brassiere. Before she could grab it, Stavros approached us and said "Come on now ladies, you aren't really going to do a striptease here, are you?"

2:00 am, The Monte Carlo Casino, Monaco

We scooted out of Caves du Puy before we lost our bras. After a quick motorcycle ride back to the yacht, we sailed up the coast and docked in sumptuous Monaco. Nico said with a grin that to live in Monaco all you need is a lot of money: Monaco citizens enjoy extravagantly high incomes. We strolled by their holiday palaces, sparkling in the starlight like colossal jewels, and saw the light-pink Palais des Princes, the winter residence of the Royal Family of Monaco. Stavros had recently attended a party hosted by Princess Stephanie and nearly suffered a black eye from a royal prince when he tried to dance with one of the prince's former paramours. Stavros said that as he was being escorted out of the palace, he vowed to beat the prince in the next Monaco Grand-Prix. Kate and I looked at each other and laughed, these Greek men were so ridiculously macho — our 'cavemen' escorts.

We headed towards Monte Carlo, one of the four Monaco quartiers, to try our luck at the famed Monte Carlo Casino. This is where the upper echelon of European society comes to play. When we reached the casino, our friends, intent on some serious gambling, headed right for the *Salon Privés* (private rooms) for some high-stakes blackjack, craps, and baccarat. The Salon Privés were quiet opulent sanctuaries for focused gamblers: the only sounds were of the roulette wheel spinning and dealers softly murmuring. Chandeliers, gilded mirrors, and drawings of bathing nymphs provided a lavish atmosphere. To truly experience the Monte Carlo Casino a large bank account is essential. We watched Stavros and Nico gamble with an indecent amount of cash, more than enough to feed a small country. Kate and I passed a few hours gambling at the craps table, nibbling on paté, sipping cognac, and rolling the dice for our handsome friends to bring them good luck. It worked. Nico and Stavros soon acquired large rolls of cash and even larger grins.

As we walked outside, a silver Lamborghini pulled up from behind the magnolia trees. A tuxedoed James Bond look-alike stepped out of the car and introduced himself as Michel. Our conversation soon turned to the gentlemen's toys. Stavros pointed to their yacht in the water below. Michel commented that it was a lovely yacht, while staring at Kate and I.

"How fast does she go?" asked Michel.

"12 knots in strong wind," replied Stavros.

"Well that's pretty impressive," Michel said, still staring at us, "but I have a Lamborghini that goes about 325 kilometers an hour."

While Stavros and Nico started to argue about the speed of their yacht, Michel winked at us, and Kate gave me a devilish look. She grabbed my hand suddenly, and we slipped into the Lamborghini. I called out to Stavros that we would be back in a short while. We were soon gliding through the gentle Mediterranean darkness with Michel. I looked at the speedometer and said to Michel, "You better make this baby go 325 — otherwise we'll have to get right back on that yacht!" Kate laughed, and the car started to roar.

6:45 am, St. Tropez Harbor

Kate and I eventually ended up back in St. Tropez, courtesy of the 'mega-yacht.' Stavros and Nico were gentlemanly about our tangential Lamborghini ride and only slightly miffed. When we returned to our hotel, a fax from my agent was waiting for me. And I soon set off for a sportswear shoot in Jamaica …

Jammin' Jamaica

Arrival at Montego Bay Airport, Jamaica,
September 26th

1:00 pm, Long Bay Beach, Negril

Finished with modeling dozens of capri pants, I had a few days to catch my breath before I headed back to the catwalk. The salty water was lapping against my toes as the couple next to me got a little more comfortable by shedding their swimsuits and dipping into the water. Yes, this was Jamaica. The famous reggae musician Bob Marley sings "No woman no cry," and I thought to myself, 'Who was he talking about?' The sun was warmly caressing my body and the gentle trade wind, known as the 'doctor breeze,' was softly touching my long hair. No woman in her sane mind would cry in this beach utopia, especially with all the fruity margaritas and tanned hunks prowling up and down the beach. "Miss would you like to take a swim with me?" A muscled Jamaican man with dreadlocks gazed down at my body, which was barely covered by my string of a bikini.

"Why would I want to do that?" I teased him a little bit.

"Uh …" he pauses, "my name is Rama. Let me show you Jamaica, yes? Okay." He answered his own request and reached down and started to pick me up with both of his strong arms.

Normally, I would have jump-kicked this guy, Thai-boxer style. But his exotic looks and peaceful energy won me over. The next thing I knew I was plopped down in the passenger seat of his jeep. I turned on the radio as he went to retrieve my towel and backpack. When he returned, he told me that he was a singer in a local reggae band and planned to cut an album in the United States. His cousin used to play the drums for Bob Marley before Bob left Jamaica to became an international star.

"Your cousin?"

"Yeah, sure. Why? You don't believe me, *mon*?"

I laughed. I stared at his huge biceps and listened to the reggae pumping on his radio. No woman no cry.

1:15 pm, Cruising by Jeep, The North Coast

Cruising towards Montego Bay, a popular resort city, I looked around and was astonished to see lush vegetation everywhere: the soil appeared so rich that if I lingered too long amongst the greenery I too probably could have sprouted leaves. Rama noticed my curiosity and gave me a quick lesson on local facts — Jamaica is a tropical island that lies roughly 800 kilometers south of Florida. Jamaica has about 2.5 million people, of which the vast majority are black, descendants of slaves who originally came from a multitude of tribes in Africa. Jamaica became independent from Britain in 1962, but the island still retains some British influences after three hundred years of colonial rule (somewhat like Hong Kong), including a tradition of tea and crumpets in late afternoons. Jamaica is well known for its *Rastafarians*, peaceful people who live simply and believe in equality and freedom from oppression for all of humanity. Rama also explained that in Jamaica, people live their lives to reggae music (it's the omni-present background music). Reggae is as essential for living as food and water. Native to Jamaica, it combines a slow, relaxed rhythm with political lyrics about oppression.

Rama was a very macho, adventurous driver. He drove so close to the edge of the road that I screamed and clutched his arm as I looked down the cliffs that led to beaches 300 meters below. I noticed a ring on Rama's finger and asked if he was married. He laughed and said, "Not too many be married in Jamaica." He explained that noncommittal relationships are most common; couples usually live together, sometimes only temporarily. Rama said that the prevalence of these living arrangements has its roots in slavery, as slaves were not permitted to foster long-term relationships, but were urged to have offspring. Nowadays, women and men often have children with several different partners, without every marrying. Rama said there are disadvantages to not getting married but also some advantages:

"After all," he grinned widely, "variety is *de* spice of life."

I teased Rama and said, "With such variety how do you keep up your energy?"

He said that he (and many Jamaican men) maintain his libido, or 'nature,' by drinking all kinds of juices that enhance his prowess. I laughed as he told me some of the names: Tear-Up Mattress, Break-Down Bed, and Front-End Lifter. He said that Irish Moss is a common ingredient in these concoctions. Remembering my friends back in Singapore who also like to preserve their virility, I told Rama that I must buy some to take home with me.

Turning from the sensual appetite to the physical, Rama then described Jamaican cuisine. Popular dishes include *jerk* chicken (made with 'jerk rub' — a paste of spices including habanero pepper), fried plantains, and ginger beer. He also said that Jamaicans make full use of their food sources, dating back to the period of slavery when they were given only the most undesirable portions, for instance chicken necks and cow feet. He told me I must try some cow feet, and I replied that I would, as long as he came to Sulawesi with me and ate stewed bat and fried forest rat.

3:30 pm, Montego Bay Public Market

Rama and I stopped in Montego Bay so he could show me his friend Dulcie's handmade Jamaican crafts at the Montego Bay Public Market. As we approached Dulcie, we could hear reggae music blasting from his walkman, and he was wearing a t-shirt that said '*Ganja* (short for marijuana) University.' Rama laughed as he slapped Dulcie on the back and introduced me. Dulcie said "C'mon let me show her around" and led us around the public market. There were Jamaican women yelling, "C'mere boopsie, I t'ink you like," and putting money deep between their breasts after a sale. (Rama said they are called 'market mammas.') There was Blue Mountain coffee, Rasta woolen tams (caps), coral jewelry, floral perfumes (many from the heliconia flower), tie-dyed clothes, brightly-painted wooden fish, *gungo peas* (which look like lima beans), sugarcane, and breadfruit. Dulcie led us to his booth full of *jipijapa* products (jipijapa is a tropical plant, commonly used to create Panama hats), including baskets, hats, and mats. All the crafts were so unique, but I was most enticed by Irish Moss, and I bought several bottles.

I thought about what I wanted to see next ... As I had always been curious about Rastafarians, I asked Rama if it was possible to visit a Rastafarian community to see how they live. Rama said, "*Cool runnings, mon.* We'll visit my friends."

6:30 pm, The Forest, Southeast of Montego Bay

Dulcie joined us, and we drove through the rainforest along a narrow, winding dirt path, the sounds of wild critters serenading us in the twilight. When we finally reached the settlement, we found that it was a spirited environment of small houses, a large bonfire, and men and women with dreadlocks sitting in a circle chatting, some smoking marijuana. As we sat down in the circle, Rama whispered to me that marijuana or 'wisdom weed' is considered to be a holy plant and is often smoked during spiritual rituals and for medicinal purposes. Perhaps to justify the use of the drug, Rama said the bible instructs, "... eat every herb of the land" (from the book of Exodus). As for the hair, Rama explained that Rastas also follow the command of the bible,

"... they shall not make baldness upon their head, neither shall they shave off the corner of their beard" (from the book of Leviticus). Rama said that the act of letting their hair grow long and free, so that it twists into dreadlocks, is in recognition of the Rastas' African roots and is in rebellion against the shorter, straighter hair of their oppressors.

I started talking to a Rastafarian sitting next to me, named RasJ, who was wearing the traditional Rasta red, gold, and green colors of the Ethiopian flag. He told me that the red color is a symbol of the blood sacrificed by Rasta martyrs; the gold color symbolizes the riches of the promised land; and the green color represents the promised land's lush fertility. He gave me some background history, explaining that Rastafarianism was established in the 1930s by Marcus Garvey, a leader in fostering black pride. (He also organized the Universal Negro Improvement Association.) The name 'Rastafarian' was chosen in homage to Ras Tafari who became the last Emperor of Ethiopia in 1930. He changed his name to Haile Selassie, meaning Power of the Trinity, when he took the throne. Many consider him to be the Messiah of Africa. RasJ says that Rastas grow their hair long in honor of Haile Selassie's sacred symbol, the lion. (The lion, like Haile Selassie, is the 'king of all beasts.') As for the history of Africans in Jamaica, Rastafarians believe that they are a lost clan, stolen from their homeland and banished into Babylon, the white power structure. Rastas can find comfort that *Jah*, God, will eventually appear and guide an exodus back to their home, Ethiopia, the Rastas' heaven on earth, known as Zion.

RasJ explained that Rastas live according to a philosophy of peace and humanitarianism, in opposition to greed and oppression of any form, just as Rama had said. From the Rastas' peaceful protest against persecution, reggae music developed. RasJ said that true Rastafarians live very simply — they study the bible, eat organic foods, and abstain from meat and alcohol. I asked him, somewhat timidly, if such a strict life also means abstinence from the opposite sex. He smiled shyly and said, "*Boopsie*, human contact is an essential of life, and *de* more *de* better!"

10:30 pm, Turtle Beach, Ocho Rios

After sharing some *bammy* (pancake-shaped cassava bread) with RasJ and the others, Rama, Dulcie, and I all headed back to the coast, farther east to Ocho Rios (another favorite tourist destination). Rama was going to sing with his band, Cool Yu Foot, at a *Boonoonoonoos*, which means 'beach party' in Jamaican. Rama said that there are boonoonoonoos in almost every Jamaican neighborhood on weekends — reggae pumps out from every village nightclub (that often is just some sound equipment rigged up in a tree). On this night, the beach was quite a scene with lighted torches and women and men sipping margaritas, getting ready for the reggae to blast. As Rama and his band started to pump reggae, the whole crowd began to *ride de riddims* (dance). I was shocked. I thought I knew a thing or two about dirty dancing but these Jamaicans, WOW! In Jamaica, dancers *wine on ah bumsee*, which literally means 'to move against a woman's bottom,' and it is X-rated! Watching the very close body contact, I was amazed that Jamaica is not a more heavily populated island. I had to fight off one guy in front of me pushing against my chest and another getting awfully close to my backside. I loved dancing with Dulcie though, as his fingers gripped my hips and his own hips pulsed against me in rhythm to the reggae. I completely lost myself in the beat of Bob Marley's reggae music.

1:00 am, The Caribbean Sea

As the last reggae set ended, the atmosphere started to get a bit amorous. There was a reggae dance contest on stage, and one young woman got so excited she peeled off her skirt and blouse and threw them into the crowd. Then the drummer of the band walked toward another impassioned tourist who had been dancing herself into a sweaty madness, took her hand, and led her to the ocean where he started gently splashing water on her. Many guys and girls with romance on their minds took his lead, finding partners and luring them into a playful bath. The shore started to become a frisky, post-reggae communal baptism. Rama and Dulcie were chasing me all over the sand trying to grab my hand but I outran them and entered the invigorating water by myself. The pulse of the reggae was still vibrating through my body, the stars were twinkling above, and a group of joyful Jamaicans were splashing around in the water with me. Had I found Zion? As the Jamaicans say, *"Everyt'ing irie."*

Jamaican Talk

Babylon — the establishment, white society.

Batty — bottom or rear end, as in "yu batty too big, mon!" (As heard from a woman who doesn't give a damn for your looks.)

Boonoonoonoos — fabulous, greatest, and beach party.

Boops — a man who keeps a woman in idle splendor (guys, watch out if a girl tells you "mi wan you fi mi boops.")

Boopsie — a woman with a sugar daddy.

Cool Runnings — no problem.

Cool yu foot — slow down, relax.

Cris — from crisp, meaning top-rate; "'im a cris, cris t'ing" (he's handsome), heard from a woman who fancies a man.

De — the.

Do — please, as in "do, me a beg yu."

Downpresser — a Rastafarian oppressor.

Dunzer — money, also known as smallers.

Facety — cheeky, impertinent, as in "Yu facety, yu know gal!" (You're rude girl!)

Fiyah — a Rastafarian greeting.

Ganja — marijuana, also known as *'de 'oly 'erb*, wisdom weed, *colly wee*, *kaya*, *sensie* and *tampie*.

'im — he, she, her, his, it.

Irie — alright, a term used to indicate that all is well; also the equivalent of "groovy," also a greeting ("everyt'ing irie?")

Jah — God, an Old Testament name popular with Rastas.

Kingman — husband.

Level vibes — no problem.

Lion — upright, usually for a righteous Rasta.

Massah — mister, derived from "master" of slave-era days and now used for any male but particularly, one in authority.

Mon — man/woman.

Naa — won't, as in "Mi naa go dung deh." (I won't go down there.)

Natty — dreadlocks, also called natty dreads.

One love — parting expression meaning unity.

Pollution — people living in spiritual darkness.

Riddim — rhythm, Jamaica's reggae has it, as do Jamaican men and women.

Roots — coming from the people or communal experience.

t'ink — think.

Wine — sensuous dance movement, body contact considered integral to a good time.

Zion — Ethiopia, the promised land.

A Trip to a Nudist Resort

Arrival at San Diego International Airport, San Diego, California, October 8th

I delightedly found out about nude recreation from a male model I met in Jamaica on the sportswear shoot. He arrived wearing a t-shirt that said "Naked Farms." I was immediately intrigued, and later spent some time talking to him about exciting nudist areas and nudism in general. He said naturists (as most nudists prefer to be called) have existed since the first human beings walked the earth. According to him, these human beings protected their bodies as necessary, according to environmental conditions. If the climate was hot, "you certainly wouldn't have seen a caveman wrapping bark around his torso." Society, and particularly the rise of organized God-fearing religions, introduced an attitude of shame toward the body — rules of modesty were constructed and nudism became generally prohibited (although somewhat allowed in young children, since they are considered pure and innocent). Naturists believe, quite contrary to its supposed purpose, that clothing is extremely aphrodisiac, serving to sexualize the body, keeping it concealed and beyond attainment.

Well, I had decided to flout societal convention and agree with my early cavemen ancestors — there would be no 'bark' for me, I wanted to take it all off. As a human being, I deserved to feel the sun, wind, and water on every inch of my flesh. So I called my agent and told her I needed a break from modeling and headed off to the Southern Californian desert. My destination was a nudist resort recommended by my model friend. The brochure they had sent me made it clear that this was not a 'clothing optional' resort as some resorts are, where you can choose whether or not to wear clothes. This was a *nudist* resort — no clothing permitted. Yippee! Everybody naked! What fun! (Actually I did get permission to wear a bit of clothing 'if necessary' as I was visiting for the first time, and not an actual nudist yet. The director said they do not want to cause any 'trauma' by forcing complete stripping during an initial visit.)

The night before my nude adventure was to commence, I wondered if the nudist community would be more progressive or less (compared to mainstream society). Would I feel more spiritual or more body-conscious? Then thinking about the latter, I started to feel anxious. I checked out my whole body in the mirror — was everything presentable? As a model, I was used to making sure my assets were in top form — arms toned, nails manicured, eyebrows plucked. But now there were a few more considerations ... As I worked myself up into a hyper-ridiculous state, I pondered this question: would my best/worst asset change? Instead of seductively shaking my hair to catch someone's eye, would I now learn to shake my left buttock? And what about the male body, which would be completely, irreversibly exposed to me in myriad forms, all its secrets, laid bare in the bright sunlight? Would this be too much? Was mystery preferable? Was ignorance truly bliss? And then I thought about my mother: modeling was exhibitionistic enough for her — the idea of me running around nude would definitely be way too much of an exhibition. This was the body my mother had spent years shielding from male eyes. And I was to undo all her efforts in an afternoon. Alas. This was certainly not the type of activity I was ready to tell my mother about. So I just told her I was going to California. I was hoping she would think 'Disneyworld.' Beyond my mother, I thought about the horror my more austere female Muslim friends in Asia would feel about my foray. Some of them weren't even showing their nostrils or a single strand of hair on their head, and here I was, about to bear potentially everything. I dreamed that night of writhing naked bodies and of my mother screaming.

The next morning I arrived at the resort, registered, paid a small fee and was told to head into the women's lounge and get comfortable (i.e. 'take your clothes off girl!') I had half an hour before my co-ed orientation session would begin and I could acclimate to just being around women until my debut (nude debutante). So there I was amongst iced tea and cookies, fashion magazines, and several other female nudies. We tittered nervously — it was the first time for almost everyone. Before long an announcement came on that Eric and Katrina, our nudist orienteers, were ready for us. (But were we ready for them?) Out from the women's lounge we sprang forth, and out from the men's lounge across the hall naked guys emerged. It was like a number from a nude musical. Everyone was looking at each other but pretending not to. 'Checking each other out' sure had a broader meaning now. But come on, how can't you look? I couldn't help but be fascinated with wondering if a guy might get a little too excited. This question was later resolved ...

We were all led into a surprisingly sedate conference room (we sat on chairs with towels) and introduced to Katrina and Eric, both young Yugoslavians. They said they had been recruited as guides because they had each grown up in nudist resorts and were 'nudist experts.' Katrina gave us an illuminating lecture on Nudist Etiquette (she was the Emily Post of the Bare Buns) and passed out laminated "Nude Manners" cards. The most interesting rules read:

1. No cameras permitted without consent of the management *(no covert pornography!)*
2. When using resort furniture or in the restaurant, please sit on a towel
3. Piercings or jewelry worn in the genital area are not allowed
4. Any person who has an infectious disease or 'open sores' is prohibited from using all facilities *(yikes!)*
5. No sexually explicit or erotic behavior allowed

Eric then offered some 'helpful hints' about nude interaction. He told us that a major concern for most men is about controlling the 'private part.' He said that it is not uncommon for a man to become aroused in a nude social scene and there is no need for embarrassment. The man and those around him can decide if it is offensive. The man should simply use sound judgment and try to ensure that no one feels uneasy. If needed, there are many discrete options: he can always excuse himself, turn over on his stomach, or jump into the pool. Eric said that one should just practice common sense as you would in any other social setting.

The orientation ended and Katrina and Eric suggested we take a look around the resort and "celebrate our newly found body freedom!" From the safety of the conference room, I peeked out onto the grounds and saw what looked like, in some ways, the beginning of the world — pre-clothing, and with all the bouncing cute butts it seemed like the advent of clothes had really been a major mistake. I was surprised that there seemed to be about as many women as there were men. I had thought that perhaps some women would think twice about removing their clothes, but not this bunch. No one seemed the least bit uncomfortable — since everyone was naked they were all on equal footing, and people paraded their nakedness proudly. Slipping out of the conference room, I walked around, observing dozens of tanned and naked women and men — both the nubile and the wrinkled — playing volleyball and basketball, paddling around on canoes, steaming in the hot tub, even tossing horseshoes! I had never been around so much nudity before and it seemed really funny, strange, and titillating at the same time. The variety of body shapes was mesmerizing — different buttocks for all!

Eric had said that the whirlpool could get pretty 'riotous,' so I decided to check out this action for myself. Along the way I saw Katrina giving tennis lessons. Everyone was playing very badly, completely missing easy shots. I guess there was just too much distraction with all the 'balls' flying around. At the whirlpool, there was a group of men and women splashing and frolicking in the water, wet and naked. There was also a plethora of conversation topics because what was usually hidden was right out there in the open. One fellow had nipple rings, and everyone wanted to know if the piercings had been painful and if the rings gave him pleasure. Eventually, a few women started to finger the rings, and after a copious amount of nipple massage, the fellow's little fella got excited. He sheepishly said, "Um, excuse me," and headed for the showers, observing excellent nudist etiquette.

Next, I decided to go for a swim in the pool. I wanted to feel the sensation of water gliding over my body. I dived in, and corny as it was, I couldn't help but feel like a mermaid with my long hair and body caressed by the water. I soon joined a water polo game with Katrina and though we were obviously not the best players on the team, we were sometimes guarded by two or three guys trying to grasp the ball, or our bodies as it seemed. Katrina and I eventually decided to reap a little revenge by tickling their bellies. As the guys were bobbing up and down in the water, aiming for their midsections was dangerous because their nether regions were in close proximity. After a brush with more than what we bargained for, the boys were becoming way too happy. Katrina and I got out of the water.

After my 'close encounter,' I decided to pick up shuffle-boarding. (I hadn't seen this being done since reruns of "The Love Boat.") I joined a group of young women who were playing with a group of guys. Amidst pushing our shuffleboarding discs, conversation soon intensified from the weather, to Katrina and Eric's relationship, and eventually to our nude female bodies. One of the boys couldn't resist saying to one woman, "Your bosom is lovely," while another offered to rub on some suntan oil for me as "Your buttocks are getting a little pink." Celebrating our body freedom was getting a little too intense.

I tried to calm the boys' hormones by having an intelligent conversation with them about nudist philosophy. Although the boys expressed interest in acceptance of the body and the ability to see people as people without all of the clothing artifice, they were also quite interested in seeing the girls from their nearby college in their natural state — the very girls that they try to ask out on dates. I thought about what an unusual town this was: you could see someone nude before you even dated him or her. Goodness!

You could also run into your mayor, your dry cleaner, or your dentist at the resort, and you would both be naked. Do you *really* want to unveil more than your teeth to your dentist; and do you really want to see your dentist reveal himself? I think not.

Katrina walked over, reminding us of the rest of the day's activities. There would be a slide show on nudity in ancient India in the clubhouse, karaoke in the rose garden, and a *canuding* (canoeing in the nude) demonstration in the pool. Later that evening, a sculptor would be discussing her latest work — the male nude (as if we needed any pointers at this point). The joviality and openness of this nude society was so refreshing. After romping around naturally, I really didn't want to resume my uniform of tight leather pants, push-up bras, and skin-tight tops I wore as a model, nor re-enter the world of fashion at all (who needs fashion when you don't even need clothes?) On the contrary, I felt like I needed to do my part in promoting nudism in the real world. I made a mental note that before I left the resort I would grab a bumper sticker I had seen in the registration office that read: *"If God had wanted us to be naked, we would have been born without clothes!"*

¡Viva Costa Rica!

Arrival at San José International Airport, Costa Rica,
November 3rd

Hola! (Hello!) ¿Cómo estás? (How are you?) Soy muy bueno.
(I am very good.) Even though I was a bit anti-fashion after my
nude adventure, an excellent assignment came up. Destination —
Costa Rica. And what an amazing country it turned out to
be. Located in Central America, about the size of peninsular
Malaysia, it sits between Nicaragua and Panama, straddling the
Caribbean Sea and the Pacific Ocean. The country leaves visitors
incredulous — Costa Ricans call it *pura vida* (pure life), a utopia
of enchanted lagunas, teeming rainforests, and grumbling volcanoes. The best of the Latin culture and tropical climates are
abundantly realized: *merengue* and *salsa* music saturate everyday
life, as do huge blue *morpho* butterflies and the fragrance of
jacaranda trees. As the sun sets, girls in silver jewelry slink by,
leaving a soft sweet memory. Out in the bush, the night is thick
with Central American jaguars stalking their prey and crayola-
colored macaws squawking.

With lush jungles, coves, and coastlines, Costa Rica is quickly
becoming a favored destination of modeling shoots. The assignment I took happened to be a calendar photo shoot. On my flight
to Costa Rica, I sat next to two Swedish models, Inga and Merja,
who were flying down with a Swedish fashion magazine. During

the cocktail hour on the jet, we all took a sip of *guaro*, the popular Costa Rican drink known as 'sugarcane fire water.' We laughed till tears came to our eyes and our stewardess quickly brought us bottles of water to soothe our throats. She said that if we ever wanted to try guaro again, it is much less painful to drink when mixed with *Café Rica* (coffee liqueur). We landed in the capital, San José, where I would spend the night, and I kissed Inga and Merja good-bye as they were off to Playa Hermosa on the Pacific Coast. Then I met up with Brigham, a British photographer, and Manuel, a young Costa Rican photographer's assistant, whom Brigham had hired to show us around and assist us on the shoot. I watched as Manuel easily lifted my four heavy bags full of make-up and swimsuits. With his splendid dark lithe body, full lips, and striking green eyes, I couldn't help but think we should use Manuel in the photos.

El Cuartel de la Boca del Monte

Brigham and I were feeling adventurous. We asked Manuel to take us to a wild Costa Rican club, and he said he knew of just the right place. Manuel led us to El Cuartel de la Boca del Monte, a frequent hangout of young *Ticos* (as Costa Ricans call themselves). The salsa band *Los Bandoleros* was playing and Manuel explained that salsa includes the Latin dances of the *mambo*, *cha-cha-cha*, *guaganco,* and *guajira.* In salsa, the male dancer is responsible for coaxing out his partner's sensuality, by caressing and adoring her body. Looking at the dancers, one thing was certain: Ticos love to dance, and they had perfected a steamy method. The dancers grasped each other's waists, buttocks, and legs in a clamp-like fashion, dancing navel against navel. Watching this passionate clutching of Ticos and Ticas, I thought to myself that I had been doing some corrupted form of dancing my whole life. This was the real romantic version and it looked like wonderful fun. As if reading my mind, Manuel grabbed my hands and before I knew what was happening, he was turning me, spinning me, and rubbing me, the inner part of our thighs touching with each step. Our bodies grew damp and warm and the salsa rhythms pulsed through my blood. This was truly a dream come true — Latin men know how to hold a woman.

I eventually needed to cool off so I walked out the back door into a small courtyard. I was surprised to see a very dark room in front of me with music playing loudly. As I entered the room and my eyes adjusted to the darkness, I noticed many women dancing on a mirrored, spotlighted stage, several wearing 'dental floss' string bikinis (called *tangas*). Some of the women were also wearing long white boots up to the middle of their thighs. They weren't doing salsa, but a type of dance I had never seen before. They moved at an amazing pace, in a unique Latin American style that paid a huge amount of attention to the buttocks. The women bent down with their heads to the ground and thrusted their buttocks up and down. Some even did handstands against the wall, while still energetically shaking their bottoms. I had heard about a Latin fetish for buttocks and this was a clear illustration of such obsession. Everyone in the audience was entranced. I, too, was hypnotized — the pace of the dancing and the writhing bodies were almost animal-like. As I was watching the women, a hostess came over to me and said that if I liked this, I should go around the corner to see a male dance performance called *maripepinos*. The dance gets its name from a famous Costa Rican cabaret dancer, *Maripepa*, and the Spanish word for cucumber, *el pepino*, as it is a dance emphasizing the pelvis!

Soda Palace

Unfortunately, I couldn't talk Brigham and Manuel into going to the maripepinos, so we headed to a *soda*, a cheap cafe specializing in Costa Rican *bocas* (snacks). We went to the Soda Palace near the Parque Central, where the 1948 independence revolution from Spain was plotted in between gulps of guaro and *gallo pinto* (the national dish of rice and beans). Latin American revolutionaries — how sexy. Political discussions still filled the air, as did romantic murmurings and *mariachi* songs. Manuel invited a mariachi singer over who called himself Don Juan. He serenaded us with his guitar while we drank *refresco*s (fruit drinks) and ate *torta espanola* (a giant omelette). When we finished the meal, we asked Manuel about other hotspots in town, and he said his favorite area is San Pedro, known for its vivacious bars lining the streets — sounding similar to Singapore's Boat Quay. But the most hot-blooded part of town according to Manuel is Gringo Gulch, with a plethora of frisky clubs and plentiful late night carousing ... Since we were *gringos*, we simply had to go.

The Bikini Club

In Gringo Gulch, we went to The Bikini Club which lived up to its name, with all the cocktail servers wearing bikinis. The music was salsa, and everyone was dancing close. We ordered some tequila shots and were about to dance when a tall Costa Rican man leapt up on a stage, introduced himself as Fernando, and asked for volunteers for a girls-and-guys wet t-shirt contest. The crowd started buzzing, girls looking down at their chests, wondering if they should enter the contest, guys flexing their pectorals and biceps. Manuel tried to nudge me toward the stage but I smiled at him and declined (the last thing I wanted to do was be ogled by a crowd of drunken *gringos* — I could do that at home). Four young women volunteered and Fernando led them to a dressing room at the back. They returned, bra-less in white t-shirts, and took the stage. Llenas, a dark-haired girl from Costa Rica, went first. As Fernando poured a pitcher of ice water over Llenas, to everyone's amazement she grabbed her breasts and instructed Fernando *"¡Darme mas papasito!"* (Give me more papa!) The wide-eyed audience craned their necks to watch Fernando pour more water over her. Next up was Angel from California. She waited patiently as Fernando doused her with water, and then grinned devilishly while lifting up her shirt, showing her naked chest to the audience. The crowd was cheering thunderously while two more young ladies, Elisabeth from South Carolina, and Maria from Costa Rica, followed Angel's lead and stripped off their tops to show themselves off. Llenas was now getting a lot of pressure to remove her t-shirt, cries of *"¡Que se la quite!* " (Take it off!) filled the air, but she refused and eventually won the contest. Apparently, guys enjoy seeing naked breasts but not on the women they like the best. Does this reflect the victory of the male's socialized side ('Take home a nice girl to mother') over the male's lustful side ('Hmmm, I like seeing her bare chest!')?

The fun wasn't over yet as Fernando next asked for handsome guys to take the stage and put on the white t-shirts. I looked at Manuel's strong and toned chest, squeezed his hand, and pushed him up front towards Fernando. Manuel looked anything but excited to participate and I thought for a minute he was going to make a run for the door. But he bravely got on stage, as did two Americans. Once the guys changed into the shirts, Fernando said he needed some girls from the audience to help the guys show off their muscles. Girls were jumping up and down squealing to be chosen, and Fernando had no choice but to pick the several girls who stampeded the stage, nearly knocking him over. As Fernando poured water over the boys' chests, their 'assistants' sensually massaged the boys' muscles. And as they became more confident, the boys all performed their own little strip-teases, slowly removing their shirts and dancing erotically, or more accurately, trying to. Manuel, so tan and boyish, easily won the contest, and the rest of the night the ladies were swarming around him, trying to entice him into slow dances.

The most insane part of the night occurred a few hours later when Fernando told the dancing crowd that the first person to run around the room naked would win a daytrip to Panama. Some bold Frenchman removed all his clothes, sprinted through the room, and collected his prize on stage from Fernando, completely naked. Soon after it was *Buenos Noches* (Good Night) for me with kisses on the cheeks for Manuel and Brigham.

From San José to the Caribbean Coast

The next day Brigham, Manuel, and I rose early and headed for Cahuita on the Caribbean Coast for our photo shoot. We munched on *pain de maíz* (corn sweetbread) and drank delicious *café con leche* (coffee with milk) in the car as we passed by beaming Costa Rican children on their way to school. Once we left San José, our route was through the mist-laden cloud forest of the Braulio-Carrillo National Park. A couple of hours into our drive, Manuel suddenly told us we were entering a hazardous area of frequent landslides. Worse yet, if a car is stuck in a landslide, it is dangerous to get out because of the poisonous snakes in the area: Burmese pythons, king cobras, and *terciopelos* — the latter are the creatures responsible for more than half the poisonous snakebites in Costa Rica. Hearing that, I had a flashback of that horrifying picture of the snake with the boy inside its belly in Sulawesi. Starting to feel queasy with the danger of landslide and snakebites, I asked Manuel to slow down. Further along, we thought we saw the Irazu Volcano, reaching 3,432 meters. The volcano last erupted on March 13, 1963 — a date coinciding with John F. Kennedy's diplomatic visit to Costa Rica. Greetings, Mr. President!

The road soon carried us through forested slopes and tranquil, humble villages. As we passed through a village named Cimarrones, Manuel explained that the name means 'runaway slaves,' and we guessed that the village had been a haven for slaves who escaped from Caribbean plantations. When we reached the shore, part of the Mosquito Coast that stretches from Guatemala to Panama, the turquoise blue of the Caribbean took our breath away. Driving south along the plains, the fertility of this land of plenty was evident — there were sugarcane and banana plantations, farms growing macadamia nuts and cocoa beans, and small armies of trucks carrying the haul to markets and ports.

Cahuita

We found our way to Cahuita, a funky beachtown full of the international-backpacker crowd and popular for its glassy waters, bleached sand, and sheltering palms. The scenery offered such an ideal tropical setting that we shot rolls and rolls of film. It was lovely splashing through the water and lounging under the trees.

We tried a few creative shots — I took off my top and used palm leaves for coverage, making use of the 'island girl' effect for good measure. This caused quite a bit of a stir among the small crowd that had gathered to watch the shoot. They taught me several Spanish phrases that afternoon such as *"Darme tu autografo"* (Give me your autograph) and *"Hey Mamita que hembra"* (What a babe).

Puerto Viejo

Although our Cahuita friends invited us to stay for a night beach bonfire, we decided to head to Puerto Viejo which was rumored to have the most festive nightlife on the Caribbean Coast. As we were driving south, Manuel said that in Puerto Viejo nearly everyone walks around barefooted. This relaxed lifestyle, coupled with the laid-back atmosphere, has enticed many Europeans and North Americans to move there and open small cafes and adventure-tour companies. And sure enough, at the first beachside bar we hit, we met a small crew of gritty California surf veterans. Most of them were living in Cahuita and were happy to take advantage of the leisurely pace of life and the gnarly Costa Rican waves. Before long, some Costa Rican guys came by with their guitars and we all sang Beatles songs together, communicating with each other through the lyrics and big grins.

Then we went down to La Bamba, a dance club, where we could hear the hypnotic Latin/Caribbean beat of *lambada,* music similar to salsa. There were many dreadlocked Rastafarians there, and the scene reminded me of Jamaica. I also noticed several female tourists with Costa Rican men. Manuel explained, as he looked at me, that it is customary for American and European women to 'enjoy' the local men. Manuel said it is so common that some Costa Rican men assume that visiting women will indulge in 'free love.' Well, this was certainly an interesting intercultural dynamic, particularly with regards to Manuel and I. I was a bit intrigued ... In the meantime, however, Brigham and I started doing the *macarena*, a dance that originated in Latin America. We jumped on the bar and macarenaed next to a guy who nearly fell off with the excessive shaking of his bottom. In the midst of the cool ocean breezes, pumping Latin music, and friendly Ticos, someone started chanting *"¡Viva Costa Rica!"* (Long live Costa Rica!) And we all joined in.

Ski Weekend

Arrival at LaGuardia Airport, New York,
December 12th

Over New Year's back in New York, I happened to meet my high-school boyfriend, Daniel. He told me he was planning a weekend ski trip to Park City, Utah, and he invited me to join him and his friends. I was booked to fly out to Colorado for a ski goggle ad in early January, so I decided I would hop over to Utah afterwards.

Utah has become a favorite destination of the world's *powderhounds* because of the amount of *powder* that falls there. Utah's car license plates gloat "The greatest snow on earth." And they have a point — the snow there is feather light and copious, falling about fifteen meters per season. Within Utah, Park City is the hip town. The U.S. Ski Team has lived and trained there for twenty years, and the city will host the majority of the ski events in the 2002 Olympics, including the slalom, giant slalom, and ski jump. But many people who hang out in Park City don't even bother to ski. They come for the *après-ski*, including the independent film crowd who descends for Robert Redford's annual Sundance Film Festival.

Arrival at Salt Lake City International Airport, Utah, January 9th

I flew into Salt Lake City, the capital of Utah, early on a Thursday evening and was met at the airport by three boyish fellows. There was Daniel, tall and rosy-cheeked, and his old college friends Bryan and Jonathan, both well-built and outfitted in serious ski gear. The three of them looked like members of the Olympic Ski Team, and I immediately knew that this was not going to be a ski-for-a-few-hours-and-hang-out-in-the-lodge scene. We jumped into Bryan's jeep and drove through the immense Rocky Mountain Ridge towards Park City. Even in the dark I could see the mountains, black against the night sky, hovering and encircling us like gentle welcoming giants. A few of the slopes were sparkling with twinkling lights for night skiers. When we reached Park City, we went straight to Hana's, a Japanese restaurant, for sushi and sake. I met Bryan and Jonathan's girlfriends, Rebecca and Georgia, who were both athletic, bubbly, and dare I say, curvy in their ski sweaters. As Jonathan made a toast, he mentioned that both of the couples were high-school sweethearts who were still in love. Then he looked at Daniel and I, and said, "And what about you two?" We looked at each other and both groaned.

We ate rows of California rolls and drank enough warm sake to make us feel immensely cheerful. I told them how I had grown to like *fugu*, Japanese blowfish, from eating at sushi bars in Asia. The attraction of fugu is the danger that comes with eating it; some parts of the fish are extremely poisonous and can cause paralysis and death within minutes of swallowing. Eating fugu can be a bit of a metaphysical experience because each bite could be your last and the fragility of your life becomes perfectly clear. Other qualities that make fugu attractive include a prickly, tingling sensation from trace quantities of poison and aphrodisiac properties. Of course the latter tidbit immediately interested the boys and several plates of fugu were hence ordered. After the last bite of fugu (fortunately, the sushi chef was having a good night), we were off to Bryan and Rebecca's condominium which was nestled in the mountains. The boys displayed fine boy-scouting skills by building a roaring fire in the living room. Soon, everyone was drinking hot chocolate and snuggling as the effects of the blowfish kicked in.

The next day we headed to Wolf Mountain, which has a summit elevation of 2,750 meters and 63 trails. We organized all of our gear as we arrived — sometimes the main difficulty in skiing is keeping track of skis, boots, poles, goggles, and gloves. Suited-up, we finally skied over to the chairlift where the excitement of the people in line was kinetic. It was like being with a group of pre-teens waiting to get into a pop-star concert. The snowboarders were particularly thrilled.

Snowboarding is a 'snowy' hybrid — part surfing, part skateboarding. Snowboarders cruise down the mountain on something that is essentially a skateboard without wheels, ripping out moves through a precise balance of body weight. Snowboarders are also known as 'shredders' and are usually young, sassy, and wear baggy, often unflattering, gear. In contrast, skiers are usually older, wealthy, and more elegantly-outfitted. There is a subtle underlying tension between snowboarders and skiers. Some skiers believe that snowboarding doesn't belong on the ski slopes, and some snowboarders think that skiers are close-minded and uptight. It is 'punk mentality' railing against 'old elitism.' Taunting sometimes occurs between the two camps, for instance a snowboarder may stop suddenly in front of a skier and 'mistakenly' spray him with snow.

According to Bryan, most of the snowboarders at Wolf Mountain are not casual amateurs. They are 'hard-core' athletes, extremely passionate about snowboarding. They either live in Park City and snowboard every day, or fly in as much as possible. I spoke to some of the snowboarders in line and found that many of them had quirky nicknames — there was Grandmaster X, Shred, and Pink Wax. Pink Wax wasn't in the chairlift line for long — she went straight to the front of the line. A Black Pass affords this privilege, but it doesn't come cheap, costing several thousand dollars. Soon, we hopped on the chairlift and started floating up the mountain. Underneath us was skiing mayhem — there were poles and skis littered on the slopes, their owners submerged in ski banks, snowboarders somersaulting off cliffs, and a chorus of whoops and hollers. My stomach started to feel queasy with fear as I looked up at the mountain ahead of us, looming huge and steep …

We arrived at the summit, with thousands of meters of vertical powder awaiting us, and headed towards Bearclaw Run, a 'black diamond' trail for expert skiers ('blue squares' are for intermediate skiers and 'green circles,' also known as 'bunny runs,' are for beginners.) I hadn't skied since the previous season and a super nervous adrenaline charge started pumping when I saw the very steep slope and realized there was only one way to get to the bottom. And that was to ski. The two couples immediately jetted off down the slope, flying through the snow leaving a trail of powder spurting behind them. Next Daniel and I started off. I cruised through my first taste of the snow and a fleet of endorphins started pulsing through my body. My brain was in complete ski revelry. 'Wow this is so fun! I'm flying, I'm free, I'm invincible!' And then, *SPLAT*, I was face first in the snow, my arms buried, and my left ski was sliding rapidly down the mountain. Daniel, witness to my pitiful start, quickly caught my runaway ski and brought it up to me. I removed my face from the snow and saw that my ski pants had a jagged rip in them. I had to get serious. I put my ski back on, remembered the techniques from ski school as a kid (lean forward, keep your knees together, don't lose your cool), and started cruising.

By mid-morning, snow started to fall, and by the afternoon it was so deep we started skiing insanely fast because of the powder cushion. I dived into the snow, zipping and zigzagging through sweet-smelling pine and spruce trees, fantasizing that the trail would extend indefinitely, a snowy passage down North America. As we reached the bottom, we sprayed each other with snow and then raced to the chairlifts so we could do it all over again. Each time I descended, the lustrous snowflakes, the lofty green trees, and the big sky brought pure joy.

For lunch, we stopped at the ski lodge where we sipped cocoa with whipped cream and consumed major quantities of black bean chili. Rebecca said that she was skiing out of control on the last mogul run and she felt certain she was going to end up head first in the trunk of an evergreen tree. Bryan and I were discussing if the skier we saw gliding through the dense woods was really Alberto Tomba, the flamboyant Italian slalom master. No one wanted to linger over lunch too long. We zoomed back to the lifts, warily eyeing the position of the sun in the sky, calculating our remaining number of runs (sunset being literally a grim prospect on the horizon).

By the time darkness did finally descend, we were exhausted and headed back to the condominium. We took off the layers of ski clothing and jumped into a hot tub on an outside deck, with full view of the purple sunset behind the mountains. Bubbles massaged our tired muscles and we all looked like true mountain folk with our cheeks and noses red from the brisk Utah air.

Feeling refreshed, we headed into town for some après-ski, and ended up at Moose's Pub & Grill which, Bryan told us, is the most happening spot in town. Ski bunnies were out in full force, dressed in pink and powder-blue sweaters, showing off their mountainous breasts. Hulky ski instructors swaggered around telling stories of escaping avalanches and surviving 150-meter cliff jumps (a few guys sported casts on their limbs — I guess they didn't make every jump). We had some cocktails there and then headed to an outrageous party hosted by Park City's social elite. There were live Las Vegas showgirls serving gin and tonics and Picasso paintings in the art gallery. But the lavish surroundings didn't interest us quite as much as the heaps of snow that we heard were predicted for the next day.

Powder did fall the following day. And as we approached the mountain to ski again, there was talk about coming back the next weekend. As much as I was bewitched by Utah's rad slopes, I couldn't immediately return. I had already made travel plans in Thailand …

Trek through Thailand

Arrival at Don Muang International Airport, Bangkok, Thailand, January 17th

"Immediately return to your seats ladies and gentlemen, we are experiencing severe turbulence," shouted the Singapore Airlines stewardess. We had left Singapore for Bangkok an hour earlier and our plane had been bobbing and lurching in strong winds over the Gulf of Thailand. It felt like Godzilla had us in his clutches. I left the cockpit where the pilots had been consoling me with "It's under control" and returned to my poor friend Jessamyn who was sitting with her head between her legs moaning and nauseous. The plane was rolling from side to side, the hour was late, and we were terrified. After what seemed like an eternity, we finally landed in Bangkok's Don Muang airport.

We quickly realized that our frenzied entry was an appropriate introduction to the throbbing, dizzying energy that is Bangkok. As we took a taxi into town, we marveled that even after midnight traffic was thick: *tuk-tuks* (three-wheeled taxis), mopeds, motorcycles, cars, and buses swerved and honked mercilessly, while people blanketed the streets in an escape from their sweltering apartments, buying all sorts of Thai delicacies from vendors and savoring the night. Bangkok was booming! Everything about Bangkok is intense, even its name: officially known as *Krungthep*

— *phramaha* — *nakhonbawon* — *rathanakosin* — *mahinthara* —
yutthayaa — *mahadilok* — *phiphobnobpharaat* — *raatchathaanii*
— *buriiromudomsantisuk*, the name is usually shortened to
Krungthep, city of angels. Our taxi was heading for Khaosan
Road, the legendary backpacker area.

I was traveling with Jessamyn, an old friend and a model from
New York. We had both taken two months off from modeling to
explore Thailand — to the chagrin of our agents. Mine had sternly
told me, "You should work constantly in your prime years and
save for your future." But we wanted to travel in our intrepid
youth and so we set off. We decided to do the trip the 'bohemian'
way — staying in youth hostels where we could hopefully meet
local Thai people and hip travelers rather than the same-old
models, businessmen, and narcissistic celebrities of the five-star
hotels we were becoming accustomed to. I had purposely not had
my personal assistant arrange for a car to meet us, make hotel
reservations, or select a tour guide. I did not even have my cell
phone with me. We were armed only with a guidebook and our
excitement.

Roughing it in Bangkok

We reached Khaosan Road and in our zeal to really rough it out,
we went to the cheapest place we could find. The manager led us
up the sloping stairs to a room furnished with a bare light bulb,
stained mattresses, and a trail of ants winding their way up the
sallow yellow walls. Jessamyn and I looked at each other in horror
and fled back to the taxi. I told the driver to take us to The
Oriental Hotel, the favored Bangkok haunt of blue bloods and
literary giants — writers such as Joseph Conrad and Somerset
Maugham have slumbered there. I thought we would spend a little
time acclimatizing to Bangkok before we jumped into the
backpacking scene.

After we secured our plush suite, we immediately ordered
room service and nibbled on some Thai delights like *tom ka gai*

(coconut chicken soup), *pla priaw waan* (ginger fish), and *khaaw niaw mamuang* (sticky rice and mango). Then we sent for a masseuse, who turned out to be a young, baby-faced Thai man. He introduced himself as Pira and greeted us in the traditional Thai style, with his hands held together under his chin as if in prayer, a gesture called *wai*. He looked a little timid and asked us if we wouldn't prefer a female masseuse. Quite the contrary, we thought he was the cutest thing and giggled as we told him we were not letting him leave until he had thoroughly massaged us. He looked a bit intimidated about the prospect of rubbing us down, but he composed himself and shyly cooed for us to remove our clothes and slip into the hotel's silk robes. As we laid on his massage table, he gave both of us *nuat boroan,* traditional Thai massage. He sensually and firmly worked his thumbs along the "ten main lines" of our muscles, softly whispering to us that this would help release blocked channels of energy, and could be a deeply spiritual experience. His angelic voice was soothing and hypnotic, and the touch of his fingers was so pleasurable that we were completely relaxed. Next, he told us we should bathe in hot water, and he filled up our large whirlpool, placing several pink orchids in the water. We begged him to stay and perhaps take a little swim with us, but he blushed and said he had to attend to his next client. After he left, Jessamyn and I slid into the hot water. From the whirlpool, we could see the twinkling lights of Bangkok over the Chao Phraya River. Despite the charming sight, Jessamyn's attention was elsewhere. "I'd like to stash the masseuse in my suitcase and bring him home," she murmured.

Hitting the Bangkok Streets

The next day, we woke late and hit the steaming Bangkok streets. After a few hours of walking around, my mind was reeling with images of Bangkok. First of all, *san phra phum*, spirit houses, were ubiquitous — they can be found outside people's houses, banks, hotels, and restaurants. They look like miniature Thai *wats* (temples) and house the 'resident spirit' of the building, who must be placated with offerings of food, money, incense, and flowers. Guests should ask permission of the spirit before entering a building and then pay respects again upon leaving. Along with spirit houses, we saw hundreds of smiling Thai people, everyone appearing to be having *sanuk* (fun) as they went about their daily routines. The people of Bangkok seemed to have heaps of inner joy.

We also saw many statues and images of the Buddha. Jessamyn and I learned that a rite of passage for men in Thailand is to become a monk for a short time and enter the *Sangha* (Buddhist brotherhood). A young woman, Kamolmal, whom we met at a posh gem boutique, told us that most men will be ordained as monks at some point in their lives, and the government allows civil servants to enter the monkhood for three months with pay. She said that as the tradition is so common, there are over 30,000 monasteries in Thailand. Kamolmal paused and then said, almost apologetically, that a few monks were recently involved in controversy. Since many people give large cash donations to monasteries hoping for a pleasant afterlife, a small percentage of monks had access to bank accounts in the millions. Some of these monks were accused of staying in luxury hotels, dating young women, and visiting brothels, acting a bit like rock and roll stars. Jessamyn and I were surprised, but Kamolmal added that even monks are only human, and the vast majority are completely pious "men of God."

After the monk disclosure, Kamolmal continued her revelations, telling us that in general Thais are open-minded about sexuality. For instance, homosexuality does not carry the same stigma in Thailand that it does elsewhere. Even transvestites are widely accepted, and a transvestite volleyball team won the national title in 1996 (although they were not chosen to represent Thailand internationally). Kamolmal told us that before we left Bangkok we should check out the nearby restaurant Cabbages and Condoms where we could eat in dining rooms named with birth-control themes. Jessamyn wondered if there was a 'Trojan Extra-Large Room.' I could definitely imagine a guy feeling pleased to eat there.

We left Kamolmal's boutique and munched on sate from a street vendor. We were constantly craving for more *náam manaaw* (lime soda) under the excruciating tropical heat. Jessamyn reminded me with a sigh that Bangkok is usually cited as the world's hottest city — it certainly had my vote.

More than We Bargained for

In the early evening we noticed two Thai businessmen following us. I thought maybe they wanted to sell us some gems (rubies and sapphires abound in Bangkok, many from Burma) as many young men had tried to throughout the day. We stopped and, in a very serious tone of voice, asked why they were trailing us. They introduced themselves as Kukrit and Vatcharin and meekly said they thought we were 'gorgeous' and wanted to show us around their city. We dug a little bit into their background, and they said that they both worked for the Siam Commercial Bank and had gone to business school in America, at Stanford. Okay, it sounded convincing. Warming up to them a little, I said, "Well what do we *have to* see in your city?" They laughed conspiratorially and said they had a surprise for us. We were not sure what they had in mind, but they seemed like decent guys and we were feeling adventurous.

We piled into a taxi and they asked us to close our eyes. I was beginning to feel that maybe this wasn't the safest situation for two girls to be in. We reluctantly agreed, but I told them that I knew the U.S. Ambassador in Bangkok (a bit of an exaggeration), and if they tried anything funny with us they would definitely receive some horrible punishment. After about twenty minutes, the taxi stopped and the boys said, "Please keep your eyes closed a little longer!" They escorted us into a noisy room and I thought that maybe it was a restaurant. When some rock music came on they finally said we could open our eyes. The first thing I saw when I opened my eyes was a nearly naked young lady laying on a stage catapulting an egg from between her legs. I realized we had arrived at the infamous Patpong area, the Thai playground of 'sex and sin.' I felt I should have been somewhat angry with these boys for taking us here (I had heard the shows were exploitive of young women), but as Patpong is so notorious I did want to see it for myself and form my own opinion. Out of politeness, I can not reveal everything I saw that night but I will offer this — the young woman with the egg was also able to very creatively blow out a candle; another act involved a beefy gentleman performing double-time heroics with two females (and then asking for male volunteers from the audience to join in); and a third act showcased a woman doing amazing contortions on a hanging rope, making full use of her bountiful breasts. We told the boys that this was certainly unlike anything we had ever seen before. Kukrit replied proudly, "In America there is a lot of boasting about wild sex, in Thailand they actually put it into practice." They were practicing it all right. The audience was composed primarily of large groups of Asian and European men. Vat said that most of them were probably on package 'sensual tours.' After each segment of the show, painfully lovely females would come out to the audience and lounge on some of the men's laps. After much whispering back and forth, the men would often leave their table for 20-30 minutes and then come back, rumpled and grinning, ordering drinks for everyone.

I couldn't believe that all this was' legal. Kukrit said that prostitution is technically illegal — yet the police hardly ever interfere because brothels, sometimes called 'tea houses,' are found in almost all towns. Even if the police become involved, only prostitutes and their 'pimps' can be arrested under Thai law, not clients — which seemed completely unjust. Kukrit said that it is a rite of passage for most young men to visit a brothel (quite different from the other rite of passage of becoming a monk). He said that the whole experience is so perfunctory that prostitutes often lay motionless with clients, sometimes even flipping through magazines as they 'work.' Kukrit said that a "very special treat" is a Thai *soapsud* massage, in which a masseuse soaps up her naked body, lays down on a man, and slides back and forth, wriggling and pressing herself onto every centimeter of his body, giving him total body stimulation.

As if Vat hadn't talked enough about women servicing men, he launched into an explanation of *mia noi* — the institution of minor wives. Vat said if a man can afford one, having a mia noi indicates high status and, he added with a wink, provides diversity. Kukrit broke in and said that strict rules, however, must be followed: mia noi can usually only be taken out in private, while first wives must accompany their husbands for public appearances, such as state dinners.

After all this talk about men and their pleasures, I said exasperatedly, "Well what do Thai women do for their enjoyment?!" Kukrit thought for a moment and then said, "Oh, Thai men like to satisfy women!" He said that it is a centuries-old practice for men to insert metal rods into their 'private parts' and attach different accessories, including feathers, to ensure a woman's complete ecstasy. Sometimes, gold or ivory hollow balls, with grains of sand inside, are inserted. The balls make tinkling treble tones when moving and supposedly charm a woman beyond belief. I asked Kukrit and Vat if they were personally familiar with these devices. They just smiled and asked if we really wanted to know. Jessamyn, looking very pale after the whole evening's sights and stories, replied, "No boys, that is really not necessary."

Kukrit and Vat suggested going to another 'sinful' area, Soi Cowboy, and they said late in the night some friends of theirs would be racing motorcycles in a street race, but we had to bid them *Sa-wut dee ka* (Good-bye), as we had already booked a night train south. They whined that we were *mai sanuk* (not fun), and pleaded with us to at least go with them to the Royal Bangkok Sports Club for drinks. I think they had been hoping Patpong and all of its sexual energy would serve as an aphrodisiac for us.

The Midnight Train to Paradise

With relief, we escaped Patpong and the rather clueless, self-absorbed boys, while feeling sad for the women who worked there. We knew that the majority of the women came from poor villages. And with limited education, they had few economic options. Most of them were working in Patpong to support their families. Many were so young, it was heart-breaking. (At the same time, we also felt a bit guilty, because in all honesty it was somewhat fascinating to watch the bizarre acts.) We wished we could liberate all the women for a vacation on the idyllic islands of Koh Samui and Koh Phangan, where we were heading next.

We had booked a train on the well-worn route to the south, and were eagerly anticipating the romance of a night sleeper car. Our 2nd class ticket (we *were* trying to rough it out) provided us with a small compartment shared with two other passengers — a guy from Belgium, Martin, and a girl from Singapore, Grace. There were two bunk beds, and the four of us stayed up talking most of the night. Martin, quite a handsome buck, had been a rock singer in Los Angeles, a scuba diving instructor in Israel, and served in the Rhodesian Army for a short time. Grace was an abstract math graduate student and had just spent several weeks at a Bangkok *wat* studying *vipassana* (insight) meditation. She had spent many hours in contemplation, concentrating on quieting her mind. She had stayed there for free, meditating, cleaning the wat, and eating rice with the monks. Grace told us that as we traveled further south from Bangkok, there would be more mosques, sarongs, and rubber plantations, the landscape becoming increasingly Malay as we approached Malaysia. Late in the night, as I snuggled in my little train berth, I could hear the grunting and chugging of the train as it slowly moved in the dark night through old Siam, and I felt the train's serene grandeur.

In the early morning, we arrived exhausted at the sleepy little port town of Surat Thani. Martin, Jessamyn, and I (Grace was heading back to Singapore) groggily walked off the train and arrived at the dock which was crawling with backpackers. It was a colorful sight with the backpackers' red, purple, and orange batik sarongs and bright packs in the early morning light. A small boat eventually arrived and we all climbed aboard, happy to be heading towards the isolated little island of Koh Samui.

The Islands, Koh Samui

After a couple of hours cruising through sun-dappled sapphire water, we made it to Na Thon, the main village in Koh Samui. Martin headed off to Big Buddha Beach. Jessamyn and I hopped onto a *songthaew* (minibus) to Chaweng Beach, the largest, most happening spot. When we reached Chaweng, Jessamyn and I found a bungalow right by the sea for only one dollar a night. We had come a long way since The Oriental Hotel. The bungalow was magical. Recently built from bamboo, the cozy structure was still fragrant with the fresh scent of the plant. Inside there was a little bed with a mosquito net, which because of its associations with explorers, made us feel quite intrepid. There was a communal shower, which we could use, or we could bathe in the Gulf of Thailand. We called two of our model friends, Greg and Charlie, who were doing a shoot in Tokyo, to let them know where we were, as they would be joining us in a few days. (It turned out that Greg and Charlie barely found us because Charlie was drinking a little too much Japanese sake when we called and scribbled down something almost indecipherable.)

For the next five weeks, the four of us did nothing on Koh Samui. Nothing. I called my friends in Singapore and New York and they asked, "Well what are you doing there?" and I said, "Nothing, nothing at all and it's great." Of course we were doing something, but the overall sensation was of just being alive, a bit *Zen*. Each night, Greg and I grabbed our sarongs and slept on the beach to the sounds of crashing waves and wind rustling through the palm trees. We would look up at all the stars and wonder how humans ended up on earth, and if we would someday live in other galaxies. During the day, we lounged around, drinking lots of *náam âwy* (sugar cane juice) and nibbling on sweets like *khao kriap* (sesame pastry) and *kluai khai* (sweet bananas). At night, we had seafood feasts in tiny candlelit cafes on the beach.

By the third week, I did get a teensy bit antsy and wanted to see the rest of the island. So Charlie and I motorcycled around, visiting some waterfalls and Big Buddha Beach on the north coast, where Martin from our train ride was staying. On our way back to Chaweng, we made a sharp turn, skidded on some leaves, and were catapulted off the motorcycle onto some bushes. We only suffered a few scratches, but later learned that Thailand has the world's highest death rate on the roads, and Koh Samui has the highest motorcycle mortality rate in Thailand. We felt very fortunate with our slight injuries.

After our accident, we stuck to 'water sports,' swimming in the warm gulf and lounging on the topless beaches. This was the only place that, initially, Jessamyn and I felt like we had a job to do. From too much exposure to modeling competitiveness, we became a bit riled up when we watched dozens of women parading around, proudly displaying their bodies. We couldn't resist taking part in the game: we strutted our stuff and, according to Charlie, left a wake of smitten boys and bewildered girls. Then we felt absolutely ridiculous and corrupted. We had become competitive models, exactly what we didn't want to become in the first place. And we resolved to curtail that behavior immediately.

One night after a long day at the beach, I was overcome with nausea. Jessamyn felt my head and groaned about how hot it was. She asked the owner of the bungalows to give us a lift to the local hospital. Jessamyn helped me into the back of the owner's pickup truck and I started to get scared — I was very far from any major hospital, I didn't speak Thai, and I was about to empty the contents of my stomach into the back of the truck. We arrived at the tiny Koh Samui hospital, and I was brought to a dimly-lit examining room. As a doctor (who luckily spoke English) started to inspect me, I could hear screams outside the examining room. The screams kept coming closer and closer until a screeching, bleeding man was wheeled in on a stretcher. He had apparently been knifed and was losing blood from several slashes in his stomach. My doctor swiftly stuck a needle into his arm and the man calmed down. The doctor turned back to me cool as a cucumber. *"Mâi pen rai,"* the doctor said to me (Not to worry). As he continued to examine me, I started to move in and out of consciousness and I vaguely heard the words 'malaria,' 'typhoid,' and 'influenza.' After a litany of tests, it turned out that I had a severe case of influenza. The doctor told me I had to stay in the hospital for an indefinite period of time, and that I immediately needed intravenous medicine and careful observation. Yikes! I wasn't sure if I should stay in this little hospital or fly out to Singapore or Tokyo for medical attention. I eventually decided I would stay, making it part of the backpacking experience.

I spent the next week in a crowded ward, with groaning and moaning surrounding me day and night. I was very nauseous, hot, and nearly comatose, sleeping most of the time. Jessamyn was so kind, she brought me fresh fruit and mineral water every day and spent several nights sleeping next to me on the floor. By the eighth day in the hospital, I had lost more than five kilograms. I was very weak and I did not feel significantly healthier. Somehow though, I remembered that we had to get to the next island, Koh Phangan, for a full moon party, and I rationalized to myself that some fresh air would do me good. So I simply unhooked my I.V., said good-bye to the nurses, and grabbed a songthaew back to our bungalow. Jessamyn, Charlie, and Greg were a bit aghast to see me hop out of the minibus, pale and very thin. But how could I miss the party?

The Islands, Koh Phangan

While on Koh Samui we had heard many rumors about the infamous full moon parties on Koh Phangan. The full moon party has roots in Buddhism — many Buddhist festivals, commemorating aspects of the Buddha, take place during the full moon. (For example, the full moon festival in May, *Wisakha Bucha,* celebrates the birth, enlightenment, and death of the Buddha.) The full moon party on Koh Phangan, however, has taken on its own traditions and would not completely please the Buddha: nearly 10,000 people squeeze onto this little tropical isle every month to dance all night, with some partaking drugs like psychedelic mushrooms and ecstasy.

As soon as I spent some time on the beach following my hospital 'escape,' I felt revived and quite chipper. The following day, I headed out by boat to Koh Phangan with Jessamyn, Charlie, and Greg, arriving in the late morning at Hat Rin Beach. A group of people was already dancing on the beach and they planned to boogie for twenty-four hours straight. One guy from Brazil, Raoul, told us he had arrived a week ago and quickly got to know girls from England, Singapore, Canada, and Thailand. He said he had never been so happy — spending his days wandering around the island, talking and hanging out with his international 'harem.' Charlie and Greg sighed with envy and said that we must be in paradise. Jessamyn and I left the boys to relish in their paradise while we cruised over to Layla Beach. Jessamyn had heard that it was a nude beach and she had never been to one. She was not disappointed with what she saw — we watched one naked fellow perched on a high rock curiously juggling three red balls, and boys and girls endlessly springing out of the ocean, their tanned bare bottoms glimmering with water. We also noticed a lot of German and English male tourists with young Thai girls, the rampant Patpong syndrome.

When evening approached, we headed back to Hat Rin. We could hear techno music blasting as we came closer to the beach. It was about 6 pm and the full moon mayhem was beginning. The DJs spinning the records were these super-cool Bangkok, Berlin, and London music gurus. One Bangkok DJ had dragon tattoos and a trippy coral amulet around his waist which he said gave him sexual powers. Perhaps the amulet was working because he was surrounded by a gaggle of admiring females. The theme throughout the night was hedonism — everyone seemed to be thinking, 'Here we are in Koh Phangan, it's beautiful, it's far from "civilization," there are hundreds of gorgeous girls and guys. Let's party!' As dancing, undulating bodies were living out a tropical island fantasy, several rumors circulated through the crowd: one was that the margaritas were spiked with ecstasy, another that Madonna had arrived, and a third that the police were coming by boat to break up the party. Fortunately, the police never came, although there were several boats ready to covertly take us all to Koh Tao, the next island out, if they had come.

With the crowd's exploding energy, it turned out to be a very late night. Some of the beach bars didn't even open until 3 am. By 5 am, the beach was absolutely covered with bodies, some passed out, some intertwined with other bodies. The latter group included Charlie and Greg who had indeed found paradise with two Norwegian lasses. In the end, there was just a small cluster of people left dancing, and I don't know how we had the energy (especially after my hospital stay) but Jessamyn and I managed to continue dancing, in a trance-like state, watching the sun rise for the finale. I had to lay down soon after but Jessamyn said that many bars stayed open until 10 am, serving just orange juice.

After such a sensational first night, Charlie and Greg ended up staying on Koh Phangan for weeks, but Jessamyn and I had another thing on our minds — trekking in Northern Thailand.

Arrival at Chiang Mai Airport, Thailand, March 8th

From Surat Thani, we flew up to Chiang Mai in the north of Thailand, a city that provides a convenient base for trekking and visiting hill-tribe villages. Martin, the guy we knew from our train ride, had been up north and told us to find a tour guide named Koon at a cafe near the Ton Lamyai market. Martin added that Koon is considered one of the best guides in the region. His association with the Tribal Research Institute of Chiang Mai University and his wealth of knowledge about northern hill-tribes make him an expert in great demand. We found the cafe and were told that Koon was leading a trek in a few days. While we waited for the trek, we took in the sights of Chiang Mai. We visited Bor Sang, an 'umbrella village' (where we bought hand-painted parasols made from bamboo and rice paper), and Phu Ping Palace, a vacation residence of the King of Thailand, where we had hoped to at least meet a prince or two and subject them to some 'double model' attention.

Soon the time arrived for our five-day adventure. Jessamyn and I packed up our sleeping bags, cameras, malaria pills, and loads of heavy-duty insect repellent. We met up with our guide Koon and a group of twelve backpackers, from Australia, Japan, Canada, Finland, and Holland. Jessamyn and I were abound with excitement about setting off into uncharted territory. As soon as we were assembled, Koon laid out some trekking rules: "Dress modestly (I elbowed Jessamyn because she was wearing a halter top), ask permission before photographing, and do not smoke opium." Koon piled us into the back of his truck and drove towards the highlands. We hiked several hours that day, mostly on a narrow dirt path, through gentle hills and muddy streams, past groves of bamboo trees and several waterfalls.

In the late afternoon, we started to see some signs of human habitat. We came upon terraced padi fields and could see small wooden huts in the distance. And as we got closer, we saw women hunched over under the warm sun, busy tending their rice shoots. They smiled and waved to us as we hiked by. When we reached the village, we saw some men inside their huts, many of them smoking what appeared to be opium. A few came out to talk to Koon who spoke with them in their hill-tribe dialect. Koon soon directed us to a large hut where we put down our backpacks. Several children had been following us since we entered the village, shyly grinning and jostling each other to get close to us. Jessamyn and I gave them some fruit as we walked around their village with them, exploring and taking pictures. We met an older man with black teeth and red gums sucking on 'betel nut.' Koon later told us that betel nut is made from betel vine leaf mixed with lime and the areca palm nut. The mixture is mildly stimulating, much like tobacco. With increasing contact with the outside world, most young villagers feel embarrassed about having stained teeth and choose not to chew betel nut.

As darkness descended, Koon and some village women cooked dinner over a fire — a very simple and welcome meal of hill rice and root vegetables. Koon said that some villagers eat beetles, particularly the *maeng da*, which grows up to four centimeters long. Caught at night, the beetles make somewhat of a luxury snack when they are deep-fried with chilies. Koon said maeng da is also the Thai word for 'pimp,' as the female beetle provides for the rather lazy male. After dinner, Jessamyn, myself, and two of the Finnish trekkers, Annikka and Krister (a girl and a guy) set out to watch the men of the village in their ritual opium smoking. We were all curious to see how it was done. We walked over to one of the larger huts and found a group of men chatting and preparing the opium. We saw one of the men, elderly and stooped-over, sitting on the ground mashing up what appeared to be opium paste. After mashing the paste, he scooped it up and put it in a long narrow pipe, heating the pipe with a candle. He inhaled and offered the pipe to Jessamyn, who shook her head no in response, as did Annikka and myself, but Krister grabbed the pipe and inhaled deeply. I felt a little fearful for Krister but was also intrigued by what would happen. So we sat with him watching his reactions to the opium. At first he said he felt drowsy and happy, and that the knee that had been bothering him during the day felt better. So far so good. But after an hour or so, Krister looked pale and said he felt nauseous and needed to get some fresh air. He stood up slowly and stumbled outside the hut where he started throwing up, an activity he spent most of the night doing. In his misery, Krister reasoned that perhaps the opium and his malaria medicine had been an unfortunate combination. Back in our hut, all of us, besides Krister, ended the night by listening to two guys from Australia tell scary stories about the ghosts of Northern Thailand. Soon, everyone fell asleep, nestled in our sleeping bags, exhausted from the walking and effects of high altitude.

We roamed through the Thai forest over the next four days. Koon had arranged for us to meet up with a group of tamed elephants and their owners. We rode the elephants through the forest trails while learning that Asian elephants spend up to eighteen hours a day feeding, consuming about 150 kilograms of grass per day. Koon said that about thirty years ago, wild elephants, *gaur* (large ox), and Asiatic black bears still roamed the hills of Chiang Mai. These days, one can still find some bears, but smaller animals like monkeys, snakes, and birds, whose habitats have been less disturbed by encroaching development, are more commonly seen. After riding on the elephants for some time in the heat of the day, we were tempted to cool off in a muddy stream.

Just as I was coaxing Jessamyn into the cloudy water, one of the Australians yelled, "You know there are said to be blood-sucking leeches up in these waters!" Then he picked up Jessamyn and threw her squealing into the stream. Lucky for him, there weren't any leeches. He was only kidding. Otherwise, he might have been enjoying some elephant dung in his afternoon hill rice.

Throughout the trek, we visited three different hilltribes, the *Hmong*, the *Karen,* and the *Lisu*. There was another tribe we wanted to visit but were unable to because of the distance, the *Padaung*. The Padaung has its origins in Burma. Some families live near the Thai-Burmese border, close to the town of Mae Hong Son. They are sometimes called the 'Long Neck Karen,' or more disparagingly, 'the giraffe people' because of their unusual custom — the women lengthen their necks from a very early age by wearing and continually adding brass rings to their necks. The longest necks measure thirty centimeters, and the weight of the rings can reach five kilograms. Koon said the origin of the custom has several plausible explanations — one legend has it that women deformed themselves so they would not be taken as slaves or concubines to the Burmese court. Another says that the rings protected women from tigers; and a popular Padaung myth tells of their people descending from a dragon, so perhaps women were trying to emulate the dragon's long slender neck.

Good-bye Thailand

Jessamyn and I had to leave Thailand and get back to modeling. But the country and its people had already touched us. We were charmed by their gentle spirits and desired to return soon. In addition to visiting the Padaung people, we wanted to reach the Golden Triangle, where Myanmar, Laos, and Thailand meet. And we thought we would also hit Koh Tao, off of Koh Phangan, which is probably now 'the place to be.' Or maybe we would pick up the Pan Asian Highway in Northern Thailand and take it all the way to Istanbul …

Miami Beach Party

Arrival at Miami International Airport, Florida, April 2nd

It was bikini photo shoot season, and my agent (her anger about my long absence somewhat pacified with a hand-painted umbrella from Bor Sang) sent me down to Miami Beach, Florida, to do a pictorial for a French leisure magazine, *Allez.* I was not the only one with the beach on my itinerary. Thousands of college students having their Spring Break were also flying down for a raucous beach party in steamy and sultry Miami.

Miami is a favored playground for East Coasters, jet setters, the glitterati, and the young and hip. As a vacation destination you can't go wrong here — there is stunning tropical weather, nuclear-hot nightclubs (some say this is where the foam disco was invented), and enough warm sand to make the Sahara Desert envious. Due to Miami's flagrant good looks — electric-blue sea and sky and brightly-painted buildings in shades of Easter egg colors — fashion photographers and models crowd onto every Miami-bound flight, and photo shoots are as common on street corners as traffic lights. The locals of Miami tend to be as decadent as their visitors, boasting the highest percentage of vanity license plates (spelling out nicknames like 'Hunk' or 'BabyDoll') and personal roller blading trainers in the U.S.

I arrived in Miami and was met by Jerome, a Parisian art director, and Vincenzo, an Italian photographer. We cruised around for several hours looking for the right light and location for the shoot and finally decided on a sheltered cove on Sunset Island, a secluded island north of Miami on the Atlantic Coast. In the middle of the shoot, we needed a couple of manly guys to help us out. So Jerome invited two from the crowd which had stopped to watch. Their names were Brett and Axel, and both came from Cornell University. As they flexed their muscles, they whispered into my ear about a beach party their college fraternity was having the following day ...

Mouth-to-Mouth Resuscitation

I had some time before a late afternoon photo shoot the next day so I went over to the boys' party on South Beach, one of the epicenters of Spring Break mayhem. I arrived just in time for a '*Baywatch* look-a-like contest' for women. Certainly not the most intellectual pursuit, and obviously a 'contest' designed to let the audience ogle at scantily-clad young women. Not surprisingly, hundreds had amassed to watch the spectacle. Each contestant was judged on her likeness to the female Baywatch lifeguards and her ability to perform life-guard duties — such as rescuing a drowning victim, and performing mouth-to-mouth resuscitation and CPR — all while avoiding lecherous men on the beach asking for a phone number. Many of the contestants looked quite authentic. One co-ed, Alexandra, from Duke University, had a large bouncing chest. And since her red Baywatch swimsuit was a little tight, most of her round sun-baked buns were visible, much to the joy of the men in the audience. She first paraded around the beach graciously refusing phone number requests. Then when she heard the cries of the 'drowning victim' (a guy splashing around), she grabbed a life preserver and dashed into the ocean. She swam out quickly to the victim and adeptly fought off four fraternity boys (including Brett from my photo shoot) pretending to be 'sharks' who were 'biting' on her thighs and arms. She gently swam in with the victim and laid him down carefully on the sand with the help of some other contestants. Then she knelt over him, opened his mouth with her hands, and started to perform mouth-to-mouth resuscitation. Apparently the poor boy couldn't stand the stimulation and slipped her his tongue — Alexandra won the event.

Down and Dirty in the Sand

After the Baywatch contest, most of the crowd headed over to watch a Tug of War contest between two sororities. Sororities (as well as fraternities) are usually associated with certain stereotypes that the members often cultivate. For this contest, there was the Tri Delta sorority, with the mottoes 'tri everything' and 'three times a lady.' The majority of the members present themselves as virtuous, well-groomed, and chaste — quite the 'good girls.' Their opponent was the Sigma Delta Tau sorority (nicknamed Spend Daddy's Trillions). Most of the SDTs portray themselves as affluent, exclusive, and sexy — to overly simplify, the 'bad girls.' The girls enlisted some fraternity boys for muscle power, and the object of the game was to win four pulls out of seven. These girls were very serious about winning. Each team had their feet dug deep into the sand, pulling as strongly as their manicured nails would allow, the tension visible on their faces. Perhaps they were getting their jealousies and frustrations out on the beach. ("Oh, I must beat that SDT Buffy, she stole my man!") Every time one of the teams won a pull, the losing side was subjected to a round of stony glares and smirks. After five pulls, the SDTs led 3-2. On the sixth pull, Alexandra, the Baywatch winner and a SDT, was pulling so hard that when the other team let go of the rope in defeat, she landed right in the lap of the guy behind her, Brett. Okay, something was definitely happening between those two.

I had to leave the beach for my photo shoot in the nearby Venetian Islands. We ended up chartering a small yacht to cruise around the islands, taking lots of photos in the shallow waters near shore. (There was so much seaweed I spent much of the afternoon peeling off green slime — not exactly a glamorous affair.) We did have a superb catered lunch of wine and fresh lobster as I chatted about favorite cuisine with Vincenzo, who had also lived in places all over Asia. We agreed that spicy Thai *tom ka gai* (chicken soup) is supreme 'super food,' and puts to shame the American version of the same name. When I returned to South Beach several hours later, a Dating Game was starting ...

Desperate for a Date

Basically the main reason that college students go to Florida during Spring Break is to, shall we say, 'hook up.' Especially after the titillating Baywatch and Tug of War contests, everyone was in a scramble to get a date and to be a contestant in the Beach Dating Game. The game began with the appearance of a bronzed brunette, Laura. On stage, she gave a little performance for the audience, writhing on her knees to great applause. A few overly-excited guys tried to slip dollar bills into her bathing suit. Settle down boys. Laura's job was to interview three young men and choose the one she liked best. Then they would spend two nights together at the Miami Hilton for some private fun. The first man to appear was Jeffrey, a hunky, and potentially steroid-fed fellow. As he took the stage some of the girls in the crowd started squealing. Laura asked him when he sat down, "So Jeff what is your lifetime goal?"

"I'm only interested in one goal right now Laura, and that is making you very happy."

"Well Jeff since you are on the subject of making me happy, how would you do that?"

"Women are very sensitive creatures and they really need to be touched. I want to touch you all over!" The whole crowd roared but Laura looked a bit irritated. Then, she said she wanted to meet the other two men. Hearing this, someone in the crowd yelled, "Don't be stupid, pick him!" Pete came out next, with chocolate skin, a pierced nose, and a svelte, toned body. Laura asked him, "Pete, if you really wanted to impress me, what would you wear on our first date?"

Pete thought for a moment and whispered something into her ear. Laura started to laugh.

Some guys up front shouted, "What did he say?"

"He told me he would just wear a mesh loincloth," she shouted as the crowd howled again. Laura seemed slightly intimidated by Pete and asked to see the last of the three men. Alberto came out, sun-burned, tall, and lean; he was clearly shy and not as aggressive as the others.

Laura asked him, "So what do you think of the answers from the first two men?"

Alberto looked at her and politely said, "I think those things should only be said in private Laura." Hearing this, the crowd groaned.

In the end, Laura threw caution to the wind and picked outrageous Pete. As the three men and Laura stood on the stage wrapping up the game, Jeffrey looked like he might start a fist-fight with Pete. Getting a woman was *serious* business down here in Spring Break World.

The Night Beach Games

And then as the sun descended, the night games began. Nighttime Miami is seething with energy as all hedonists get ready to engage in full-scale debauchery. Down by the beach, some local fellows started beating on Caribbean steel drums while a few fraternity boys built a huge bonfire in the sand. Soon there were fresh oysters steaming and *s'mores* (marshmallows, chocolate, and crackers) cooking on the fire. Beach cocktails like watermelon margaritas and coconut pina coladas were being mixed and sipped. Cuban cigars made an appearance, and several boys started puffing on them, but they were quickly reduced to coughing and wheezing from the strong Cuban tobacco.

A limbo game began and a long row of revelers lined up to play. The approach to the limbo stick was a sight to behold. One very Irish-looking boy (freckled and red-haired) bent back to a nearly horizontal position, bellowed, and shook and pounded on his large chest like an ape as he neared the limbo stick, clearing it easily. It all seemed quite primitive and wild, guys and girls shaking their nearly bare bodies, drums beating, and all of these lit by a dancing fire. Since everyone had spent the entire day on the beach looking at each other's barely-clothed bodies, the crowd was now trying to achieve major body contact as the drums thumped louder and louder. Dancing was just an excuse for hands to move up and down thighs, backs, arms, and chests. As I was boogie-ing on the beach with Alexandra and Brett 'dirty dancing' next to me, and Laura and Pete 'getting to know each other' in their hotel room, I completely understood the visceral attraction of Miami.

JAMAICA

REGGAE IS REGARDED AS A NATIONAL ART FORM IN JAMAICA. BEACH-FRONT PARTIES ARE A WAY OF LIFE.

A JAMAICAN BOY WITH SIGNATURE RASTAFARIAN DREADLOCKS.

JAMAICA'S NATIONAL SLOGAN.

NUDIST RESORT

CAMERAS WERE STRICTLY PROHIBITED, BUT I QUIETLY HAD THIS PHOTO TAKEN.

COSTA RICA

A COSTA RICAN COWBOY

ME GUSTA COSTA RICA MUCHISIMO!

A STRIP OF THE PACIFIC COSTA RICAN COASTLINE.

PARK CITY, UTAH

A PARK CITY SNOWBOARDER GLIDING THROUGH THE AIR.

ENJOYING THE SLOPES OF THE 2002 WINTER OLYMPIC GAMES.

THAILAND

BUDDHIST STATUE IN BANGKOK.

BUDDHIST MONKS SAY HELLO.

TREKKING THROUGH THE TERRACED PADI FIELDS
TO REACH THE FOREST IN CHIANG MAI.

THAILAND

BANGKOK'S COLORFUL FLOATING MARKET.

A WOMAN SELLING SNACKS ON THE STREETS OF BANGKOK.

UMBRELLA MAKING IN BOR SANG, CHIANG MAI.

MIAMI BEACH

SPRING BREAK HITS MIAMI BEACH.

EGADS — IS THIS A BAYWATCH AUDITION?

IN THE CLEAR, WARM WATERS OF MIAMI.

LIFEGUARDS ONLY

THE RAINBOW FAMILY

A LITTLE BACKRUB FROM FELLOW RAINBOWS.

A RAINBOW MAN AND HIS COMPANIONS.

THE RAINBOW FAMILY IN PROCESSION, PROCLAIMING PEACE AND LOVE FOR ALL!

The Rainbow Family

Arrival at Albuquerque International Sunport,
New Mexico, May 9th

I had a little time off from modeling and my friend Jennifer invited me to join her on a 'camping trip.' This was not an ordinary camping trip, but one with several thousand modern-day hippies in the middle of the New Mexico forest. I said yes after little hesitation.

I have been curious about hippies ever since my parents told me about the hippies of the 1960s. Hippies were long-haired, peace-loving, sexual and drug adventurers, considered by some to be social revolutionaries. My parents explained that the hippie counter-culture originated from several influences — the experimental music of the Beatles, the fashion from London's Piccadilly Circus (like bell-bottom pants), and the message from American folk singers such as Bob Dylan and Peter, Paul, and Mary, whose lyrics encouraged young people to make the world a better place. From these, hippies developed their unique music and fashion style and their own agenda of world peace and rebellion against war, particularly the Vietnam war. In the 1960s, men and women carried peace signs on the streets, stuffed daisies into soldiers' guns, and lived in communes, sharing everything from food to sexual partners.

Jennifer joined the 'Rainbow Family' soon after college and had been writing me provocative letters about her adventures ever since. She explained to me that the Rainbow Family has its roots in the hippie movement of the 60s and was started by members of the original love-ins of San Francisco, California. (Love-ins were mellow gatherings of music and political protest; one of the most famous was when John Lennon and Yoko Ono sang *Give Peace a Chance* from their bed to help inspire world peace.) For the past twenty-four years, the Rainbows have held an annual Rainbow Gathering open to everyone: "If you have a belly button, you can be a Rainbow" — no one is ever turned away. Rainbow Gatherings are based on the idea of tribal community — everyone shares food and possessions (no money is exchanged, except for donations) and all people enjoy equal status. In fact, there are no Rainbow leaders, all decisions are made through tribal councils. During the gathering, the Rainbows actively promote environmentalism (for instance, organizing people to chain themselves to trees to prevent logging in endangered forests) and world peace, while also offering funky music, moon-lit dancing, massage chains, and nudism.

I invited my cousin, Sarah, a crunchy hippie chick herself, to experience the Rainbow life with me. We flew into Albuquerque, New Mexico, rented a jeep and drove into the desert towards Carson National Forest, where the gathering was being held. As soon as we reached Taos, a posh artist community and ski resort a few hours from the forest, we realized that we were already in Rainbow territory. There were beautiful green-eyed Rainbow girls on the side of the road hitch-hiking — their long hair dancing in the breeze; Grateful Dead music (the classic hippie music) filled the air; and big multi-colored buses were driving by. Many buses were painted with murals: one of them showed a long-haired smiling goddess holding our green and blue planet in her hands. In another hour, we reached the forest but still had a two-hour hike into the depths of the woods. The Rainbow Gatherings are always held far from civilization. This ensures that only true Rainbow fans will actually make the trip and frees the participants from societal rules and the police.

On the hike in, three young guys walked beside us: Will, Sam, and Pete, from Colorado Springs, Colorado, who were only too happy to help Sarah and I carry our backpacks. They said they had been following the Rainbows for a few years, doing odd jobs to earn money and anything else to remain with the Rainbow Family. They said that they didn't like living in the materialistic society of mainstream America, and felt much more at peace spending their time fighting for the environment — they had been to Alaska to help clean up an oil spill and to the South Pacific Islands to protest nuclear testing. Sarah and I were quite impressed with their selflessness.

We crossed quiet pine forests, meadows, and over streams before reaching a clearing in the forest where a settlement of teepees, tents, and primitive structures made of dirt and branches had been built. Over 12,000 people were gathered in the middle of nowhere, ready to dance, sing, and love each other in Mother Nature. Everyone was divided into small camps, each with its personality, including the 'Gypsy' camp (an eclectic group of Rainbows with pagan backgrounds), the 'Peace O Pizza' camp (specializing in clay oven pizzas), the 'Granola Funk' camp (a musical group), the CALM camp (a center for alternative living medicine), the 'Nic at Night' camp (a small tobacco kitchen) and the 'Pink Fairies' camp (a camp for lesbians). A quick tour through the Pink Fairies revealed a group of friendly women sitting on each other's laps, singing songs, and playing with each other's hair. After declining the boys' invitation to share their tent, Sarah and I found Jennifer in the Granola Funk camp. She looked like the consummate hippie girl, with daisies in her hair, a pink halter top barely covering her breasts, and a long, flowing multi-colored skirt. After hugging and kissing us, she took us on a tour of the whole site.

As we walked around, I kept thinking, 'Wow, these people are cool'; there were Rainbows meditating, chanting, dancing, and drumming; Rainbows talking about politics, spiritual growth, and the future of the earth; Rainbows attending ecological work-shops and going on herb walks, and so many of them laughing and singing. Everyone was kind, welcoming, and affectionate —

particularly with hugs: Jennifer told us about the Rainbow rule that "Hugs are given and received freely." My cousin and I were a little inundated with hug requests, and a few hugs were a bit intense. One man nuzzled my neck and whispered in my ear "I love you." I was pretty sure he meant 'love' in a spiritual, ethereal sense, but regardless, I hadn't received that kind of attention since my last runway show in Jakarta. Sarah was especially curious about the prevalence of nudity. It seemed everywhere we looked we could see a naked or nearly naked guy or girl bouncing through the long green grass. Many of the nudists wore flowers around their naked limbs. Massage and body painting chains were also quite popular — people were sitting in long lines rubbing and decorating each other's semi-nude bodies. Jennifer explained that some Rainbows practice nudism to get more in touch with nature and to be physically and symbolically free from the constraints of society (Yeah, baby!)

As it began to get dark, Sarah wanted to go back to Granola Funk, the musical camp, where a P-Funk Party was starting. The word 'P-Funk' comes from the 1970s band 'Parliament Funkadelic,' led by George Clinton. Along with Curtis Mayfield and James Brown, George Clinton pioneered funk music — heavy base and slide guitar music to which your body can really move. Funk music was extremely popular in the 1970s, particularly in black dance clubs, and is much looser and juicier than 'white music.'

When we reached Granola Funk, a huge bonfire had been lit and dozens of drums were being pounded and guitars strummed; girls were going round smiling and jiggling, young punks with dreadlocks were screeching, "A P-Funk Party is the best kind of party because a P-Funk Party don't stop," and "Make my funk the P-Funk." Many revelers were smoking bongs (water pipes) which were in high demand from those without. I overheard some women imploring, "Let me puff on your bong," while many Rainbows were chanting, "Bongs for the bongless!" One older man asked a group of us if we wanted a smoke, so I took a little puff. It was so intense that my throat began to burn, my eyes started to water, and I couldn't stop coughing. Jennifer said that many Rainbows believe marijuana products are conducive to raising good feelings among people and have curative medicinal uses (similar to the beliefs of the Rastafarians in Jamaica.) Jennifer explained that some Rainbows are active in the movement to legalize marijuana and other cannabis products, and many Rainbows were next headed to the Great Midwest Marijuana Harvest Festival in Wisconsin. Yet, Jennifer said that Rainbows strongly discourage the abuse of marijuana and other drugs, and actually prohibit alcohol from their gatherings; they believe that alcohol, as opposed to marijuana, tends to make people more aggressive and sometimes violent. (The Rainbow policy is "We love the alcoholic, not the alcohol.") Before long, we were lost in the pulsating beat of the drums and enticed into the mass of sweaty bodies dancing in the moonlight.

The next morning Sarah and I woke up in our tent to the sounds of grunting. We peered outside and saw a naked long-haired couple making Rainbow love to each other on the grassy hilltop above our tent. In Rainbow world, who needs cereal to start the day? A few minutes later, Jasmine bounded into our tent and told us we should get up and relax in a sweat lodge. I had heard that steaming in a sweat lodge, a common practice among Native Americans, invigorates the body by flushing toxins from one's system. I had always wanted to try this ritual. This was my opportunity. Sarah, Jennifer, and I walked down to the river nearby, stripped off our clothes and entered the sweat lodge — a small enclosed area in the shape of a teepee. Inside, there was a small group of Rainbows sitting around a fire. Perhaps due to the sight of three young ladies entering the lodge at the same time, a couple of the boys looked so pleased I thought they might pass out from the excitement. The three of us lounged in a corner, relaxed, and let the heat seep in. It felt like some kind of opium den — smoky, everyone slightly comatose, and some Rainbows mumbling and chanting. After about thirty minutes, the lodge had done its work and I was swimming in sweat — I crawled out and slid into the cool river nearby. Sarah and Jennifer followed, and to our amusement, a couple Rainbow boys did too.

Afterwards, we all headed to the Peace O Pizza camp for lunch, where we munched on mushroom slices. At the end of the meal, as the 'Magic Hat' was being passed around (for donations), we heard the sounds of children singing and soon a parade of Rainbow children appeared. They were dressed in gaily-colored flowing clothes, holding balloons and flags, their little faces painted in shades of rainbow colors. They were so full of joy, and with all the good vibes I couldn't have imagined a more uplifting environment for a child. Conversation soon turned towards the similarities between the Rainbows and Native Americans — respect for the earth, communal living and decision-making, even the teepees, pipes, and sweat lodges. Jennifer said that she really wanted to live in the Rainbow Family full time, joining the Rainbow Trail and traveling from one local gathering to another. I too felt almost ready to join them — to turn away from the often meaningless, capitalist existence of a model, and embrace the peaceful, respectful existence of these folks.

Later in the day, we attended a planetary healing ceremony in which Rainbows focused their thoughts on world peace and harmony; all of us, numbering in the thousands, stood in silent prayer, holding hands, and repeating the chant 'OHM.' A sacred bong was later passed around and ritualistically smoked.

For the rest of the week we danced in the sun, beat on drums, joined in massage chains, and focused our energies on world peace. This lifestyle may or may not work for the whole world, but for the Rainbows, the Rainbow life is certainly filled with harmony, meaning, and joy. And, perhaps most profoundly, the fulfillment of an old Native American prophecy, "When the earth is ravaged and the animals are dying, a new tribe of people shall come unto the earth from many colors, classes, creeds, and who by their actions and deeds shall make the earth green again. They will be known as the warriors of the Rainbow."

Supermodel & Revolution

Arrival at JFK Airport, New York, May 16th

My Big Break

I headed back to New York from New Mexico to do some editorial work for a teen magazine, *Fashion Market*. The evening I returned, my agent called to tell me that she had been in contact with an international advertising agency. The agency had seen my modeling work and was interested to have me represent their cosmetic and shampoo clients for upcoming promotions. She told me that I would probably be flying out from New York within a week.

The next day, my agent called again to inform me that the ad agency was putting the beauty product promotions on hold because they had just landed a major client and were developing an intriguing campaign they hoped I would lead. The client was the PSP Group, a huge conglomerate of fashion, travel, and real estate enterprises, which had recently completed building a luxury apartment complex in Indonesia. The appeal of the campaign would center on an all expense-paid trip to Paris that one lucky apartment buyer would win. This is where I came in — the winner of the Paris trip would be traveling with me, "top international fashion model Jillian Shanebrook." I couldn't help but think how outrageous the re-creation of myself had become — that people would be enticed to spend an exorbitant amount of money on an apartment for a chance to go to France with me. I had started this whole endeavor as an experiment, perhaps now I had arrived as a 'supermodel.'

I was told that the campaign would culminate in a launching party and ceremony that would be televised all over the country. Immediately following the ceremony, the winner and I would jet off to Paris (along with a couple of 'chaperones'), where we would stay in an opulent Left Bank hotel near the Latin Quarter, in separate suites of course. I would show the winner all the glamorous Parisian sights including the Eiffel Tower, the Louvre, and the French *haute couture* runway shows. My role in the campaign sounded a tiny bit bizarre, but probably enjoyable. (If the winner turned out to be a man, I hoped he wouldn't expect me to be his actual date — only tour guide.) My agent reminded me that not only would I be sight-seeing in Paris, but I would also receive incredible exposure and publicity. She had to send the ad agency my expenses for the work, and considering the role I was playing, she felt I was entitled to a 'supermodel' fee — a $10,000 day rate and all travel and personal expenses. Ten thousand dollars. It was hard to believe I was going to make that much money in one day. I didn't intend to refuse it, but it seemed unfair that I would be paid so much for such easy work, and others around the world had to work very hard for enormously smaller compensation.

The client, PSP, wanted to start the campaign immediately and needed an alluring photograph of me. My agent said they could either use my head shot (a photo of the face — a model's 'business card') she had sent them, or I could go to Jakarta for a photo shoot within two days. I had not been to Jakarta recently and I had a multitude of other offers to follow up on — both Popular and Matra Magazines wanted to do more recent cover stories on me, while another magazine was interested in hiring me as a fashion columnist. Several television and film producers had also contacted my agent about acting in their TV shows and films. This was a great opportunity to do all of this work at once, so I decided to travel to Jakarta, leaving that night. My booker quickly rescheduled all my modeling commitments, while my agent contacted Popular and Matra to schedule the cover shoots and then informed the TV and film producers that I was on my way. Everything seemed to have fallen into place, except that it was a bit unsettling to fly there without a contract or any payment or travel expenses in advance as there wasn't enough time.

Much more unsettling was that I was walking into a very tense political situation. Parliamentary elections were scheduled to take place within ten days in Jakarta, and for the past few weeks during the pre-election campaign there had been widespread rioting throughout the country. Indonesians were angry with the economic and political situation and fed up with the lack of democratic means for changing the system — as the media was suppressed and the election process a joke. President Suharto's Golkar Party exercised a monopoly on the elections, only allowing two other parties to run, the United Development Party and the Indonesian Democratic Party, and not giving either party a fair chance. There had been a government-supported raid of the Indonesian Democratic Party headquarters the previous summer, and the leader of the party, Megawati Sukarnoputri, was subsequently prohibited from running. Suharto's party also used corrupt tactics like having their members vote multiple times using falsified documents, and threatening villagers to vote for him or they wouldn't receive development aid (also threatening students that they wouldn't graduate). They also 'counted' votes in government buildings, not in voting centers. I was alarmed by the situation as many people had already been gravely injured and some killed. But I also felt gratified for the Indonesian people that they were standing up for their right to decide their own destiny.

Arrival at Sukarno-Hatta International Airport, Jakarta, Indonesia, May 19th

I arrived in Jakarta in the late afternoon and was met by one of the ad agency's drivers, who took me to the hotel. He gave me a note from an executive of the agency, Qizong, who had developed the campaign. Qizong was tied up in a meeting and would meet me later for dinner that night. As we drove through Jakarta, I could see hordes of stern military soldiers and groups of people marching and protesting. I sensed profuse tension in the air and an ominous presence, as if something tragic might happen. I was scared, especially when I thought about Indonesia's violent political past, particularly the bloodbath that occurred in 1965 when President Sukarno was ousted and at least 300,000 people were killed in mass violence (some put the estimate as high as two million). The CIA has called that slaughter "one of the worst mass murders of the twentieth century."[2] I had seen the film *The Year of Living Dangerously* and now wondered if I was going to live it (at least for a week) ...

I felt more secure when we reached the luxurious Hotel Ibis in downtown Jakarta, owned by my sponsors PSP, and I was given an extravagant, extremely-private suite high up on the 17th floor. I took a swim in the outdoor pool and ordered some *nenas* (pineapple) and *belimbing* (starfruit) from room service, trying to unwind from the flight and the tension from election demonstrations. At eight o'clock, I received a call that Qizong's driver was downstairs and I was whisked to the Mandarin Oriental Hotel, a nearby posh business hotel. I was to meet Qizong in Zigolini's, the hotel's Italian restaurant.

When I entered the restaurant I saw a slender, good-looking fellow waving at me, and I assumed that this was Qizong. As I approached him, his eyes seemed to gobble me up and I couldn't help but think that perhaps he chose me for this campaign and flew me out here just to have a date. Over pizza margherita, I learned that Qizong was originally from Shanghai and very ambitious, having worked all over Asia in advertising. I asked him about the riot situation and he said I would be perfectly safe if I took a few precautions: take private cars everywhere, don't go out

---

2 U.S. CIA, *Research Study: Indonesia — The Coup that Backfired*, 1968.

after dark, stay in central Jakarta, and if surrounded by a rioting crowd, do not get out of the car. Then we discussed the shoot the next day. He said it would be very quick and painless, a couple of hours at most, considering the skills of the photographer, Darwis Triadi (one of the premier fashion photographers in Indonesia), and of course, the model. I told him I had plans to meet with several producers throughout the week, and he said he knew most of the directors and producers, and that the film, fashion, and advertising circles were very incestuous. He then beamed and said I would become extremely well known after this promotion and like a domino effect, I would be immensely sought thereafter. As I had realized earlier, my career trajectory was indelibly linked with publicity.

As we were leaving the hotel, a woman approached me and asked, "Are you the model, Jillian Shanebrook?" She introduced herself as a reporter from the *Jakarta Post* and said that she wanted to write an article about my modeling work in Asia. "Could I interview you?" I took her business card and said I would consider her request. (It was flattering but a bit disturbing that she had somehow tracked me to the Oriental Hotel — I assumed she had followed me from the Hotel Ibis.) As Qizong drove me back to the hotel, he advised me against the interview. My working visas in Asia were not settled yet and he thought I shouldn't advertise the amount of work I was doing and money I was earning, lest government officials complicate the process further. As he dropped me off, he told me I should come over to his house for a swim sometime during the week, as he had a superb pool and jacuzzi that I would really enjoy. I couldn't help but wonder if he had more than a swim in mind.

Jakarta after Dark

Late that night I met up with a Singaporean girlfriend of mine who was living in Jakarta. Angela was charming, as always, with her soft, calm voice and peaceful disposition. She suggested we escape all the riot tension and unwind at a disco in the back streets of

Glodok Plaza. We found the disco and entered a very dark space (which fortunately provided anonymity) with loud thumping music — a slightly unsettling ambiance. There were many young Indonesian girls and guys and foreign businessmen in the crowd. Several girls were dressed rather scandalously — micro-minis, tight t-shirts, and platform heels. Angela and I remembered how we used to change into similar outfits once we were out of our mothers' sight, probably just as these girls had done.

We danced a while and soon two Indonesian girls approached us to ask for my autograph. I obliged, and then they asked if they could give me a kiss. Why not? The first girl planted a kiss on my cheek, as I had expected, but the other girl smooched me right on my lips. I was very surprised and confused. Was this an Indonesian custom? The two girls grinned and the bolder one slipped me a card with her phone number. Then both of them walked off into the crowd. Angela started to laugh, and as I turned towards her, I noticed that everyone on the dance floor was staring at our little spectacle. Yikes! (I hoped I wouldn't be in the 'tabloids' the next day in a 'romantic encounter' with this girl.) Angela and I couldn't stop talking about the girl for the rest of the night — who was she and what exactly did she have in mind?

Ad Campaign Shoot

The next morning when I dined in the hotel's restaurant, I sat with some Dutch businessmen who thought it quite hilarious that they were having breakfast with the hotel's 'spokesmodel.' I had to agree that the whole situation was pretty preposterous. Soon after breakfast, Qizong's driver took me to Darwis Triadi's studio, a huge bungalow hidden behind groves of bamboo and eucalyptus trees. There were nearly thirty people there, including stylists, photographer's assistants, lighting experts, and executives from the ad agency. I felt a bit intimidated, probably because I was being paid so much money, but no one seemed to notice my jitters. The crew made me up, put me in a few different outfits, asked me to pout for the camera, and then fed me lunch. It was an extremely professional shoot and the job was done in no time, just as Qizong had said. Darwis was a darling to pose for with his very laid-back and relaxed manner. Before I left the studio, he asked me to return for a private sitting for his own portfolio. As the driver drove me back to the hotel, Qizong said that within a couple of weeks, my picture would be splattered all over Indonesia — on billboards, in magazines and newspapers, and on television. It seemed very surreal and a bit overwhelming. He told me his assistant would bring my payment over to the hotel that evening.

Riots

That afternoon I went to the offices of *Dewi*, a hip magazine for young women, and met with the editor, Bu Retno. She was fabulously chic, with a well-tailored power business suit, flawless make-up, and crisp haircut. She reminded me of Anna Wintour, the legendary, super-stylish editor of the American edition of *Vogue*. With all of Bu Retno's sophistication, I started to feel nervous (and also aware that I needed to 'power up' my own somewhat sophomoric wardrobe in order to play in these big leagues). She had seen my columns in Popular and Matra (where I recounted my travels, including my adventures in New York City, the French Riviera, and Miami), and flattered me with an invitation to be a fashion and lifestyle columnist for Dewi. I considered her offer but eventually decided that I didn't have the time to produce another column with my modeling schedule.

I arrived back to my hotel suite in the early evening, and reached safety just in time — Mbak Tety, Qizong's assistant, called to say that there were major riots in the streets and she couldn't come over with my payment because it was too dangerous to travel. Soon after I got off the phone, I heard loud sirens. I looked out the window and saw mobs of angry and frantic people running through the streets, throwing bottles and smashing store windows. I could also see fires burning throughout the city. I was definitely staying put inside the hotel that night! I canceled a dinner appointment with Pak Singh, a young TV-and-film producer. Mas Heriyadi, the freelance photographer, soon called to see if I was safe, and said he wanted to immediately come over to keep me company. I told him I was absolutely fine and a bit exhilarated by all the revolutionary vigor.

Risking life and limb, Mas Heriyadi decided to come over anyway. Even with our tense interaction back in Yogya, I actually liked Mas Heriyadi — he was very humorous and skilled in photography. After having met legions of photographers, I knew that for a significant percentage, it is in their nature to try to unclothe models as much as possible. As a model, this type of photographer is simply an occupational hazard, and the best defense is to remain empowered enough to say no. We had some Singapore Slings together downstairs in the hotel bar and swapped stories. He said that he was about to stage a large photography exhibition in London which included a series of the photos we had shot in his hotel room back in Yogya. (I assumed minus the topless shot.) As it became later in the evening, the rioting was still in full swing, and Mas Heriyadi asked if he could sleep in my suite for the night. Oh my. I might have forgiven him for the topless incident, but we certainly weren't going to have a sleepover! Fortunately, the crowds dispersed within a couple of hours and Mas Heriyadi finally left, with a little prodding.

Popular Cover Story

The next day, Bu Ani, Popular's associate editor, sent a car for me. I headed to the Popular offices and was happy to see Bu Ani and Mas Mujimanto, the senior editor, again. They said they were delighted to put me back on the cover because of their readers continual requests for a repeat. Hearing this, I have to admit that I felt a bit like a 'star.'

Bu Ani had arranged a shoot at a luxury resort, Klub Vila Delima, in South Jakarta. A young Indonesian model, Evie, came with us. On my first Popular outing I had been the young unknown tagging along with the television star; now suddenly I was the famous 'it' girl. Evie was inquisitive, asking me questions about the shoot, and she made me feel like an experienced pro. The two of us changed into bathing suits inside a little cabana, and as I zipped her into a black spandex bikini she looked striking with her slender gazelle legs and smooth creamy brown skin. Bu Ani made us frolic in the pool, directing us to flirt with each other and press our bodies together. At one point, we lounged on the deck and her assistant sprayed water onto us — I could practically hear Bu Ani yelling "wet and wild" (it got very corny) while the photographer shot his rolls.

Afterwards, Bu Ani and I had some lunch and she advised me on my career like a thoughtful aunt, telling me to move to Jakarta, develop my *bintang* (star) status and dazzle *sinetron* (the TV and film industry in Indonesia). We also talked about some upcoming columns of mine — she thought Costa Rica and Manuel, the photographer's assistant, both sounded dreamy.

Charlie's Angels

That night the city seemed calm, and Pak Singh, the producer I had canceled on the previous night, called to reschedule. He sent a car over to take me to his production studio, Starvision. I dolled up in my modeling uniform (silk top, mini-skirt, heels), hoping it would double as 'movie star' attire. A large jeep soon arrived downstairs and the bellboys in the lobby teased me that I must be the most popular girl in Jakarta with cars constantly picking me up. On the way to Pak Singh's office, I chatted with his driver (a talkative Indonesian lad) as we zipped through the Jakarta night.

We reached Pak Singh's office and I went upstairs to a swanky pad — full of black leather sofas, mirrored coffee tables, and slick editing equipment. Pak Singh greeted me with a kiss on each cheek, exclaiming how lovely I was in person, and introduced me to several TV and film executives, including Ravi, an associate producer at Starvision. As Pak Singh was finishing up a few business calls, I had a monotonous conversation with Ravi, who went on and on with compliments about my appearance. Certainly it was nice to be flattered, but with Ravi hardly making any attempt to get to know me — my inner person — I was beginning to feel like a non-person, just a 'shell.' Then I started to get depressed about how shallow and dehumanizing the entertainment industry could be (just as I had felt when I first started modeling). Yet I was also a willing participant, putting in effort to 'doll' myself up for the meeting. The irony was that I couldn't get my foot in the door unless I presented myself in a certain way, but once I was there I wished there was more substance than just preoccupation with appearance. When Pak Singh finished up on the phone, we all headed out to a Chinese restaurant, went straight to a sumptuous back room, and talked business.

We had a lavish dinner, including a large platter of lightly sautéed shrimp that were still alive and jumping (apparently they wiggle in your mouth and are quite a delicacy, but it seemed a bit cruel). With shrimps dancing between their teeth, the execs got down to business. Pak Singh said he was currently casting for a new female action series, *Three Angels*, based on *Charlie's Angels* (the 1970s American action show about three sexy investigators, led by Farrah Fawcett). He asked me, "If I offered you a role with a long-term shooting schedule, could you do it?" He proposed casting me as one of the 'angels' and he said shooting would start in six weeks. He was very accommodating — if I couldn't begin filming that quickly he would fit me in later, in the middle of the shooting season, as the girls' 'friend from America,' appearing in episodes for one to three months. "If we have an understanding I can fit you in, after all the Director is God!" (I was fairly sure he meant 'God' in terms of his control over the storyline of his show. But later, I thought more about his comment and realized that in societies where people place their hopes and dreams on celebrities — almost all 'modern' societies — the individuals who hire and direct them may often feel omnipotent, and in some sense, they are.) I asked him about the daily shooting schedule, and he said the usual workweek would be five days, ten hours a day, filming twenty-six episodes in six months. He would arrange all my housing, visa paperwork, work permit, and pay me as an 'A' class artist. I told him I would seriously consider his offer.

Later that night, after Pak Singh's driver dropped me off at the hotel, I was giddy thinking about playing the lead in a television show. But I also felt cautious — did I really want to enter the world of acting at this point in my career? I would have so little freedom and control over my time compared to my life jetting all over the globe as a model. I was confused. But I also knew that compared to the serious dilemmas people face every day, this decision was pretty minor.

Television & Film Producers

The next day, I met with the rest of the top TV and film producers in Jakarta, sweeping from one appointment to the next. I hadn't had time to set up all the meetings in advance, but once I walked in, they seemed to recognize me and set aside some time to meet with me. I felt very powerful — and it was fun. These big shots were actually excited to see little old me.

I first went to Intercine, the smallest production company on my 'short list,' to meet Pak Soraya. He was a bit wary to cast me. He had a bad experience in the past with a Canadian actress who had left Indonesia in the middle of shooting a feature film. As I was leaving, he said to me in a serious voice, "You have to be very sure you want to act in my films and live here in Jakarta for several months!"

Then I went to Rapi Film, the production company that was the most well-connected internationally. I met Pak Samtani who had just returned from the Cannes Film Festival, and he bragged to me about how his films were now being marketed in Europe and America in addition to Asia. His office was energetic and bustling with a multitude of *Rapi Film* posters lining the walls, in which I could recognize dozens of Indonesian starlets (many whom I had seen on the covers of Popular and Matra). He said he was looking for foreign talent, and casually asked me if a role that included 'intimate' scenes would be acceptable. Hmmm, that sounded rather amusing — I replied that I was interested.

My last stop was Multivision, the most established and successful production company in Indonesia. This was the only place I felt a bit intimidated. The office was extremely modern and refined, with a battalion of rigid security guards and smartly attired receptionists. This time instead of being led in immediately to see the producer, I had to wait at least fifteen minutes. (I could gauge the hierarchy of directors by how long it took to get in to see them.) I was finally escorted into the office of Pak Punjabi. I found it fascinating that the four directors I met were all Indian, a sign of how dominant the Indian film industry, Bollywood, was in Asia. Pak Punjabi had a snazzy office, photos of himself with President Suharto and plaques and trophies from film and television awards lined the walls. He said he was in the midst of traveling, having just returned from Cannes and heading soon to Las Vegas for a Mike Tyson fight. He suggested that we meet up in Las Vegas where we would have plenty of time to discuss upcoming film projects. We started to talk about dinner plans when his secretary suddenly buzzed him. He picked up the phone, listened briefly, and with a look of alarm told me that a group of rioters was approaching the building and we needed to leave immediately.

More Rioting

Pak Punjabi led me and the entire office staff out a side exit, and once we were on the street, I could see a huge mass of shouting people about a block away. Miraculously, a lone taxi was driving by. I stopped it and several of us jumped in (the rest of the staff were rushing to their own cars). But before the taxi was able to drive away, a group of rioters reached us and started beating on the trunk of the taxi with their fists. The taxi driver slowly accelerated, and we eventually broke free and made it to the highway. I had been around crowds of excited fans before but I didn't think these rioters wanted my autograph. My nerves were certainly shaken. When I reached the hotel, I tried to meditate but ended up going for a long swim to calm down. Somehow Mbak Tety made it over that night with my payment in cash. She looked frazzled and relieved to hand off several thousand dollars to me and free herself of the responsibility of carrying it. I wasn't sure what was more dangerous, having it in riot-stricken Jakarta or on the streets of New York where I was heading next.

Stuck in Jakarta

I woke up the next day feeling very grateful that I was leaving that night. When I first arrived, I thought I might extend my ticket to pose for some shots with Darwis, go for a swim with Qizong, and network with film producers on a leisurely schedule. But after getting caught in the middle of a riot, I decided it was not the best of times to be in Jakarta trying to conduct business. I would be on a flight out after a morning cover shoot with Mas Driego, the Matra photographer. Downstairs at breakfast, however, my Dutch businessmen friends (who I had breakfast with earlier in the week) said they had heard rumors that rioters had formed a barricade on the road to the airport, and the airport was closed indefinitely. I immediately called Singapore Airlines to find out if the airport was open and if my flight was still scheduled to leave. They said the airport was operating and the flight was running, but for some reason they could not find my reservation on their computer. They told me that the next available seat wasn't for several weeks as hordes of people were fleeing to Singapore until the elections were over. I started to feel panicky. It was so stressful in Jakarta. I absolutely had to escape. How could my reservation have gotten lost? I pleaded with Singapore Airlines over the phone to reinstate my reservation but they were unyielding, saying that my only recourse was to come down in person to their office — a lengthy drive away — and plead my case. But Mas Driego was coming over any minute for my cover shoot. Oh my! The stresses of a covergirl. In a panic, I telephoned Angela and told her that if she wanted to leave the country, she had to try to find a plane ticket immediately. Then I called my assistant back in the States and she said she would call Singapore Airlines in New York about my reservation.

Matra Cover Story

Mas Driego soon arrived and started setting up for our shoot. His concept was 'A Lingerie Fantasy.' It was not an ideal concept for me, considering the last time I shot lingerie in Indonesia Mas Heriyadi had pressured me to remove my bra. But I felt too frazzled to argue. In my worried state, I robotically put on some lacy panties and a brassiere, and he took some shots of me lounging on the bed and gazing out the window. If Mas Driego had asked me to go topless, I think I would have strangled him because of how tense I felt about my prospects of escape from rioting Jakarta. Luckily he didn't. Towards the end of the shoot, my assistant called and said she had straightened everything out and I had a new reservation. I cooed my gratitude into the phone and felt immensely relieved. Hearing that news, my heart completely wasn't in the shoot anymore. My only concern was in getting to the airport.

Escape

I packed up, said good-bye to Mas Driego, and raced to the airport (luckily not encountering any rioting crowds or barricades). I made my flight and breathed a sigh of relief once I was up in the air. I didn't realize the full scope of the violence that had occurred until I read a candid news report. The campaign violence lasted for a full month with more than 300 people killed, many in fires and traffic accidents.

Arrival at JFK Airport, New York, May 25th

Opportunities

During the several months after the Jakarta trip, I hosted a NY television show, posed for an Everlast sportswear ad, shot a film in Ireland, attended a couple of *Playboy* Magazine parties to 'network' with celebs, and performed one of modeling's rites of passage — auditioning for Baywatch (Eerk! My agent begged me). In between this flurry of activities, I sorted through the different opportunities in Indonesia, my excitement tempered by the tragedy that had occurred. I decided to turn down the Charlie's Angels role because I would have had to move immediately to crisis-stricken Jakarta, and that just didn't seem too appealing.

Mas Driego sent me some prints from our shoot and wrote that some of the Matra editors thought the photographs too racy for use in Indonesia. I also received the Popular cover story. Upon examination, I thought the pictures turned out decently except my breasts looked unusually huge in the cover photo. The angle of the shot and the padded swimsuit had strangely transformed me into some kind of mammary giant. I endured weeks of teasing from my friends. Bu Ani told me that Popular would be sending a journalist to Paris with me to cover the ad campaign trip and I would be featured in their next calendar (a Jakarta printing company was also in pre-production for a 'Jillian' swimsuit calendar). I ended up receiving loads of fan mail from the Popular story. Here is a typical letter:

Dear Jillian,

OK, first time I would like to apologize if I invade your privacy. In my country there is a entertainment magazine called *Popular* and there was Western woman picture weared desire and sexy bikini called Jillian Shanebrook. Was it you, Jill? OK, if it is true, I would like to ask you the question "Would you mind taken picture by *Playboy* or *Penthouse?*"

That's all and best regard.

The fans always want more.

As for the ad campaign, the billboards and other media publicity were in place. According to Qizong, the ads looked fabulous and the apartments they advertised were selling rapidly. By the end of the summer, the apartments had sold out months ahead of schedule, and Qizong excitedly reported that it was one of his most successful campaigns.

I corresponded with all four producers discussing potential film roles, and I also came into contact with Pak Tanzil, a director who was about to open a multi-million-dollar media center. His would be the first integrated and largest multimedia facility in Southeast Asia. He invited me to play a leading role in his next film, a science fiction feature that would start shooting in a few months. I accepted. With my enhanced celebrity appeal, I heard from Coca-Cola Amatil Indonesia and Pepsi-Cola Indobeverages (the local Coke and Pepsi subsidiaries) about representing them. I also started planning a 'Glamour Girl' clothing line and exercise video series with McCann Erickson, a global ad agency.

Intermasa Publishers in Jakarta contacted me as well. They had been following my columns and were eager to publish my modeling and traveling adventures in book form. By Christmas though, my editor was hospitalized, apparently due to stress. And by January, Intermasa said they "couldn't afford paper anymore." What happened?

Economic Crisis

As I was reviewing my options, Indonesia and Asia in general were in serious turmoil. After the riots, with President Suharto as expected the victor, political and economic stability were predicted to return to Indonesia. Yet in July, when it became necessary for Thailand to devalue the *baht*, currency devaluations started to spread across Asia, particularly in Malaysia, South Korea, and Indonesia. Over the following months, the Indonesian *rupiah* took an incredible nosedive — from a rate of 2,200 against one U.S. dollar in late August, to 10,000 in mid January, to an all-time low of 16,750 toward the end of January. The currency devaluations and subsequent decline of these economies was swift and merciless — in a matter of months economists went from touting the 'Asian miracle' to lamenting the 'Asian economic crisis.' There is still much controversy over the origins of this crisis. Was it a result of critical defects in the Asian social and economic institutions? Was it financial hysteria on the part of investors? Was too much money entering economies unable to absorb it? Had the 'Asian miracle' been an overly optimistic title?

Whatever the causes, the IMF (International Monetary Fund) stepped in with a strict regiment of reforms for the Asian economies, including an elimination of restrictions on foreign investment, cut-backs on state subsidies, and the dismantling of monopolies. Some economists were deeply critical of the proposed reforms, arguing that the IMF (largely controlled by the U.S.) was using the crisis as an opportunity to debilitate its Asian counterparts and mandate a Western capitalistic system, and that the reforms would only pose new difficulties and prevent these countries from exercising economic sovereignty. Some argued that the Asian system was basically sound and required only limited modification, not the 'draconian' changes demanded by the IMF. While in Thailand and South Korea, the IMF reforms were generally swiftly implemented, both Prime Minister Mahathir in Malaysia and President Suharto in Indonesia were slow in responding to the reforms, stating that they desired to implement their own national strategies.

Whether Suharto was affirming his right to guide his nation without foreign intervention and/or acting out of self-interest (for instance, he stalled closing insolvent banks that his family controlled — and there was the sticky issue of the supposed billions of dollars he had stashed in foreign bank accounts), foreign investors lacking faith in his efforts, lost complete confidence in the rupiah. With a huge, accelerating corporate debt (most companies had sizable foreign currency loans, and as the rupiah devalued, their debt grew) and the uncertain future of Indonesia's political leadership (Who would be Suharto's successor?), investors pulled money out of Indonesia, and the rupiah could not rebound. The situation became desperate: people lost their jobs, there was a dramatic increase in the price of food and other essential items, and amid all this, there were rising human rights violations. The Chinese minority in particular was targeted for looting, robbery, and murder by mobs and rioters. (The ethnic

Chinese are often targeted as scapegoats for Indonesia's economic problems, suffering the stereotype of being disproportionately wealthy. In reality, the Chinese are legally blocked from entering many professions — including medicine and politics — and thus find occupations as shopkeepers, factory workers, and owners of small businesses.) Indonesian companies rapidly went out of business, for example, 70% of Indonesian newspaper publishers were unable to print their news because of the price of paper, and thus my failed book deal with Intermasa Publishers. The progression of the crisis threatened economies in Singapore, Hong Kong, and Japan (which was already having problems of its own.) The global economy was also affected: as the demand for imports in Asian countries decreased, lay-offs and downsizing became necessary in overseas operations of multi-nationals. (The Kodak company alone retrenched 10,000 people citing a lost Asian market.)

On a personal level, all of my Asian projects were postponed on top of the termination of my book project. I reasoned that any day the situation would improve, the currencies would bounce back. And every morning immediately after rising, I would check the internet for the latest exchange rates and news updates. Within a few months, I realized I was as helpless as those in the Far East. I had to step back and let the region recover. My thoughts and prayers were with the Asian people. This crisis put the triviality of modeling into even sharper perspective.

Epilogue

As we look at Indonesia in the 21ˢᵗ century, we see a country facing immense challenges, from rescuing a gasping economy to eliminating Al Qaeda training camps.

Politically, Indonesia has undergone some democratic transformation, and yet the country is largely controlled by the same elite of fifty years ago. Months after the onset of the economic crisis, Suharto resigned under mounting pressure and was replaced by B.J. Habibie, Suharto's vice president and protégé, who many believed was simply Suharto's puppet. Incensed by Suharto's nepotistic replacement, riots and protests continued for months. Free elections were eventually held for the first time in forty-four years in October of 1999, in large part due to the strength and courage of Indonesian students who demanded a democratic political system. Abdurrahman Wahid was elected but was largely unable to heal the country's inert economy and resolve separatist and religious conflicts. Adding to Indonesia's problems was the unwillingness of Suharto to go quietly. Soon after Suharto's resignation, there were a series of bombings in Jakarta, including an attack on the stock exchange that killed 15 people. These acts were attributed to Suharto and his family, apparently aimed to destabilize Wahid's rule. Wahid repeatedly received votes of no confidence from his parliament and was impeached after only twenty-one months in office. His vice president, Megawati

Sukarnoputri, took the office (making quite a comeback after having been forbidden from political position by Suharto), completing a full circle of Indonesian politics of the last half-century, as she is former President Sukarno's daughter.

Indonesia has now finally escaped from the shadow of its Suharto-era. (Suharto's son, Tommy Suharto, was recently captured after having eluded arrest for ordering the assassination of the judge who sentenced him for the Jakarta bombing campaign. Suharto himself is incapacitated after a series of strokes.) But the rumors flying around Megawati are ominous. She is largely viewed as a figurehead with limited intellectual ability and has been quoted as instructing the military (still under fire for its human rights violations in East Timor) "not to worry" about human rights in its quest for national unity.

The events of September 11th have particularly grave significance for Indonesians. Indonesia is the largest Muslim nation in the world, and is home to many extremist Islamic groups (who long before September 11th were inciting violence in northern Sumatra and the Molucca Islands). It is believed that hundreds of Al Qaeda fighters have been trained in Sulawesi, in central Indonesia, and that sleeper cells of Osama bin Laden's network are readying for action. Megawati's government has publicly denied the existence of these groups, while Indonesian Muslim leaders have condemned all arrests of Islamic militants and asserted that the United States is leading a conspiracy against Islam. Megawati must appease these powerful Muslim leaders in order to avoid a civil war (90% of Indonesians are Muslim), while at the same time eliminate any threat of Islamic terrorism and pacify her Western allies.

The global economic slowdown following September 11th has left a poor Indonesia extremely poor. Although the economies of South Korea, Thailand, and Malaysia were able to revive and fundamentally recover following the Asian economic crisis, Indonesia never did. Consequently, Indonesians are suffering the consequences of a depressed world economy on top of the lingering effects of the economic crisis. The majority of Indonesians remain in abject poverty. Though having escaped the economic crisis, Indonesia's neighbors have felt the economic fallout from the terrorist attacks: Singapore is in its worst recession of 40 years. Malaysia and Thailand are in a recessionary environment with decreasing growth and increasing unemployment. The South Korean economy is the sole survivor, rallying largely through foreign investments and exports to China.

As for myself, living and traveling in Asia and the rest of the world has afforded me an incredible adventure. My travels have given me an understanding that there are many ways to live one's life on earth. With this understanding comes the realization that although we all exist in a certain societal framework, we can each choose our own path. Based back in New York, I missed my teaching days in Indonesia. So in between modeling jobs I am teaching English to New York immigrants. What has impressed me the most in meeting people from around the globe is how similar human beings are. We are all here on the same planet, with the same problems and joys – we laugh, we weep, we get excited about romance, good food, and achievements; we eventually become old and die; and through all this each one of us tries to find peace and do work that will make us feel that we have not lived in vain. I believe the most noble and lasting deeds are found in helping each other, regardless of nationality, ethnicity, or any other constructed division. Whether or not we share the same values or religions, we can take to heart what the Dalai Lama once said, "There is no need for temples, no need for complicated philosophy; our own brain, our own heart is our temple; the philosophy is kindness."

Travel, meet your fellow humans, and be kind to each other. I will tell you about my new adventures soon.

Photography Credits

Cover:
Courtesy of Karim Zandieh

Yogyakarta:
(top) Jillian Shanebrook
(mid) Julie Shanebrook
(bot.) Thomas Fahrbach

Bali:
(top) Jillian Shanebrook
(bot. l.) Thomas Fahrbach
(bot. r.) Jillian Shanebrook

Singapore:
(top) Courtesy of Singapore Tourism Board
(mid) Courtesy of Singapore Tourism Board
(bot.) Courtesy of Singapore Tourism Board

Malaysia:
(top) Courtesy of Malaysia Tourism Promotion Board
(bot. l.) Gabriel Bellman
(bot. r.) Courtesy of Malaysia Tourism Promotion Board

New York:
(top) Isaac Schild
(bot. l.) Jillian Shanebrook
(bot. r.) Isaac Schild

Indonesia:
(top) Jillian Shanebrook
(mid) Jillian Shanebrook
(bot.) Thomas Fahrbach

The French Riviera:
(top) Courtesy of French Government Tourist Office/
      Hill & Knowlton, NY
(mid) Courtesy of Monaco Government Tourist Office
(bot.) Jillian Shanebrook

Jamaica I:
(top) Gabriel Bellman
(bot. l.) Gabriel Bellman
(bot. r.) Gabriel Bellman

Jamaica II:
(top)   Courtesy of Jamaican Tourism Board/ Foote Cone & Belding, NY
(bot. l.) Courtesy of Jamaican Tourism Board/Foote Cone & Belding, NY
(bot. r.) Courtesy of Jamaican Tourism Board/Foote Cone & Belding, NY

Nudist Resort:
Gabriel Bellman

Costa Rica:
(top)   Jillian Shanebrook
(bot. l.) Gabriel Bellman
(bot. r.) Jillian Shanebrook

Park City, Utah:
(top)   Courtesy of Park City Mountain Resort/Lori Adamski-Peek
(bot.)   Thomas Seery

Thailand I:
(top)   Thomas Fahrbach
(bot. l.) Thomas Fahrbach
(bot. r.) Jillian Shanebrook

Thailand II:
(top)   Courtesy of Tourism Authority of Thailand
(mid)   Jillian Shanebrook
(bot.)   Courtesy of Tourism Authority of Thailand

Miami Beach:
(top)   Julie Shanebrook
(mid)   Julie Shanebrook
(bot.)   Tony Giese, Courtesy of Jiloty Communications

The Rainbow Family:
(top)   Jillian Shanebrook
(mid)   Jillian Shanebrook
(bot.)   Jillian Shanebrook